K
)

I hope this will
inspire
Love, Mmatshilo

Hearing Visions, Seeing Voices

HEARING VISIONS, SEEING VOICES

MMATSHILO MOTSEI

First published in 2004 by Jacana Media (Pty) Ltd.
5 St Peter Road
Bellevue, 2198
Johannesburg
South Africa

Reprinted May 2005

ISBN 1-919931-51-1

Cover design by Adele Prins

Typeset in Trump Mediaeval $^{10}/_{12}$

Printed by Formeset Printers

See a complete list of Jacana titles at www.jacana.co.za

Table of Contents

"Indeed, while Motsei acknowledges many wise men and women (Maya Angelou, Don Mattera and Credo Mutwa to name a few) some of the most profound reflections are her very own ... In reading her book, one comes to know and love the spirit that wrote it."

– Jacqui L'Ange, O Magazine

"It is this motivational voice trying to persuade us all what to do to achieve our dreams that continues to resound in one's head and to beat in one's heart after one has read this book."

– Lisa Combrink, The Sowetan

"This book is full of warmth and compassion ... One of the beautiful moments in this book is when she is chosen as a healer and how she embraces her calling as a healer. The descriptions, the language, the pictures she paints of this experience are very moving. This book is one of those that stays with you long after you have put it down."

– Nosipho Kota, Daily Dispatch

"The pages of this heartfelt book reveal a fiercely proud Motsei, both as a woman and as an African ... It's heartwarming, wonderfully earnest and certainly inspires the reader to look further into African culture as a way of spiritual enlightenment."

– Denise Slabbert, Longevity

Dedication

To those who come from my womb
My biological children
Katlego, Kgalalelo and Onkgopotse
And
My non-biological children
Across villages and townships
Who are connected to the
Heart of my womb
Through the cyclical rhythm
Of the Moon

Acknowledgements

There have been so many (visible and invisible) who accompanied me on this journey.

My aunt, Mme Kubele Motsei Beetsi Motaung is my eternal spiritual guide. She not only keeps the fires of our ancestors alight; she taught me to pray and urged me not to fear the light. My beloved parents, Rantebo and Boitumelo Motsei love me without conditions. Whenever difficulties threatened to bury me, they always offered unconditional emotional and material support. My siblings Ngao, Ramoloi, Manyane and Serake for giving me a firm sense of belonging. Lebohang and Matlhodi, thank you for the sisterhood. My children (biological and non-biological) Katlego, Kgalalelo, Onkgopotse, Kgosietsile, Okgabile and Tumisang for opening my heart to the small wonders of life.

My dearest circle of love and friendship: Nthabiseng Mogale, for staying connected no matter what; Bongani Madondo, a dear friend and fellow writer for listening to me read from the manuscript and encouraging me to take a leap; Joanne Fedler, for her love across the Indian Ocean and through trials and tribulations; Makgathi Mokoena, for eavesdropping on some of my most turbulent and tearful conversations with my gods; Julia Kim and Paul Pronyk, for their admiration and love.

My publisher Maggie Davey for her abundant spirit, my editor Janet Sheldon-Heeg for reading the manuscript amidst caring for wilting tomato plants and a butternut vine. Angela, your publicity role is only beginning but my life is richer and better filled with your zest for life. Working with a team of women in giving birth to this book has been truly magnificent.

Finally, I reserve special thanks for all whose paths have crossed with mine. Thank you all for having shaped my life and for letting me shape yours. Last but not least, I remain indebted to rural women in various villages for infusing their African Humanism into my western feminist principles. I am blessed amongst many to have these women as my life coaches.

To my ancestors, your love and care is a blessing in my life.

Homecoming

I am in the bush in a thatched house, with butterflies and a mosquito net as my curtain. I am in the house in which this book was born. Outside, just a few metres away from my room, there are snakes. Despite my deep fear of them, I nevertheless find myself asking for their guidance and inspiration in the writing task I have set myself.

As a healer who has spent a significant part of her life running away from herself, could it be that my fear of snakes is rooted in the difficulty I have in embracing my spiritual calling?

African legend regards snakes as powerful creations associated with healing and ancient knowledge. Unlike Biblical teachings, which portray the serpent as a source of evil, doomed to crawl on its belly as a punishment from God, ancient earth-based teachings revered the snake as a medium of healing and a helper to the Goddess. The snake's cyclical shedding of its skin is perceived as symbolic, a metaphor for the cycle of birth, life, and death in which we humans also participate. At the heart of this cycle lies the willingness to conquer fear and embrace a path to love, truth and light.

This book is an insider-outsider look at my life, with all its beauty and imperfections. It is a story of contradictions because:

I am modern and traditional,
Western and African,
masculine and feminine,
body and spirit.

It is the chronicle of my journey towards healing and acceptance of my spiritual gift. It is the story of a girl child born of a family of healers and chosen against her will to receive and live out the legacy of healing. Disempowered by Christian National Education and ensnared by the comforts of modern life, I at first made endless and fruitless attempts to disown the gift. Given the choice, I would have opted for a career as a musician – I would have liked to be a saxophonist or a guitarist. But although the thought still makes me wistful, if I had become a musician, would I be here, conquering my fears and writing this book?

Why are we so afraid of not being afraid? What makes it so difficult for us to look ourselves in the eye? It is because if we do, we come face to face with our own greatness. Why are we afraid of our greatness? Because it confirms our Godness; it is evidence that we are our divine source. The courage to heal and live life in spirit while in the flesh indicates our acceptance of our essence and magnificence. Having spent so much time and energy running away from myself, I am now ready to confront my fears and ask the most dreaded questions: Who am I? What have I come here to do?

With these questions in mind, I press the button on my CD player and the room is filled with the sound of the Temptations classic "Hey Girl". I have heard this song so many times before. I have even danced to it with my vibrant daughter, Kgalalelo, who sang along and danced with an unselfconsciousness and freedom that any adult would envy. It has been a pleasure and a blessing to be guided by my daughter's light. It has also been hard to face parts of me in her; the parts of me that I have been struggling to embrace. She is a giving child who is ready to accommodate others; an energetic and frank girl who seems to know exactly what her mission in life is. Because she appears so open and independent, when engaging with her one tends to focus on her exterior and overlook the child within. Living with her has helped me to give attention to my own inner child. As a girl growing up, I was so much like her; outwardly strong and independent, yet inwardly fragile and sometimes lonely.

Being raised as a girl destined for greater things in life has in many ways robbed me of the licence to be vulnerable. I found myself unable to learn the art of loving and being loved unconditionally. Throughout my schooling, I was one of the best. It was only when I excelled and received attention from my teachers and parents that I felt wanted and loved. Being a highly achieving little girl in a society that devalues women brought out the best in me, yet took away my right just to be. In my adult years, I have continued to make harsh demands on others and myself. As a gender activist, I have equated vulnerability with non-achievement, and so taken it as a sign of weakness. On the few occasions when I have gathered the strength to be weak, those around me have assured me, "We know how strong you are. You'll get through this". Fulfilling societal expectations of who I am, I used my work to bury my vulnerability, and went all out to rescue and fix the world, not realising that I am the world. As a healer, I tended to other people's wounds while my own were left gaping and bleeding.

Yet I have learnt to be vulnerable again. As a friend of mine once said to me, "Mmatshilo, you don't have to be strong all the time. Just let that heart break a little". Once I was ready, as if to prove the saying "When the student is ready, the teacher appears", the universe was loving enough to present me with endless heartbreaking situations. In the midst of my pain and confusion, the Goddess reached out to me:

> Safe in the Bosom of the Goddess
> I rock like a little girl
> Sucking her thumb
> Nursing a bruised knee after a fall
> From the Bosom of the Goddess
> I wail in pain, only to
> Fall into a deep slumber
> That dries away my tears
> Safe in her Bosom, with her
> Tender hands to hold me
> I learn to break a little
> To make room for yet
> Another life experience
> It is in her Bosom that I
> Become an innocent child
> Ready to love again without fear
> As she mends my torn spirit with love
> I know that it will be okay

Yet as I come closer to achieving my own peace, I find myself wishing for peace for all of South Africa. Peace and love – a tall order, one might say, given the violent and conflict-ridden world we live in. Incorrigible dreamer that I am, for a moment I pretend that I live in a different

South Africa – a South Africa where all African mothers are well fed both physically and spiritually, able to produce enough milk for their babies. I pretend that South Africa is a country where you would never see groups of spiritually shattered African men waiting along the road for a white man to pick them up in his truck to offer them a job, and thereby a sense of purpose. *Setlhare sa mosotho ke lekgoa* – a lie that we no longer utter, but continue to live. I yearn for an Africa where no mother, her baby on her back, waits at the gate of a construction site in bad weather for a man who has never laid eyes on his child. I wish and pray for a continent full of parents who love themselves enough to love and care for their children. Loving oneself enough gives the strength to nurture others.

I believe we all long for warmth, love and care. The world is crying out for a sense of spiritual connectedness. Yet we forget that heaven is here on earth – *legodimo le mo lefatsheng*. Earth-bound, we tend to perceive heaven as a place remote and high above us, which we get to inhabit only once we die. Yet heaven is in the here and now. Without doing so consciously or understanding, we interact with angels every moment of our lives. When we look into another's eyes, we are greeted by a reflection of the divine. Every human being is an embodiment of the highest and greatest form of existence, and yet we live our lives preparing to go to heaven "someday", ignoring the fact that we can enjoy a heavenly life on earth. We don't have to wait for our flesh to be buried in the earth before we ascend to heaven – we have the capacity to experience the majesty of being human angels living a spiritual life in the flesh.

As I write the opening chapter of this book, I feel blessed to be in Limpopo, furthering my studies in soul-building as taught by the uncertificated custodians of cultural knowledge. Having spent the day with rural women, often referred to as the poorest of the poor, I am privileged to acknowledge their abundant spiritual wealth. I recognise in them a sense of worth and dignity that many of our generation of women have lost. They are full of life; in fact, they are life itself. As we sat together today beneath a *morula* tree, their babies stayed close to the circle, each returning from time to time to its mother to receive the reassurance of a word, smile or touch, and I was reminded of the saying, "It takes a village to raise a child". These wise and dignified human beings are my teachers and I am honoured to be their pupil.

Many of the leaders of my generation who are in government, business and other spheres come from these simple beginnings, having been raised by these humble yet tenacious women. In close contact with the earth and therefore speaking the language of the soul, which the majority no longer understand, these women are often perceived as silent and voiceless. Lacking access to formal education, they are often mistakenly taken to be uninformed and uneducated. Those who take this view wonder whether these "uneducated" women are capable of educating the young and preparing them for the future, and feel that feminism can surely have no roots in such poor African soil. Yet we come from a long line of strong African women with a passion for life, although they may not have spoken out publicly. As Africans, we have experienced what it is like to be raised and touched by women who are powerful in their silence. Our undocumented life stories are pregnant with the teachings of our mothers and grandmothers.

Drawing from a limited documented African herstory, I feel the spirit of Queen Modjadji in the sacred northern parts of South Africa. I draw strength from Ambuya Nehanda, who led the Shona in a war of liberation against the British. I celebrate the spirit of Me Katilili, a woman who organised her Kenyan people against the British in the early twentieth century by refusing to pay taxes and perform forced labour.

Indeed, we come from a long line of powerful female ancestors. A return to their legacy requires that we re-learn to decipher the language of the Soul. Opening ourselves to their guidance requires that we truly listen to the language of the Spirit, and no longer hear it as just a faintly remembered whisper. Opening our lives to their gifts requires that we stop theorising about the African Renaissance in abstract terms during conferences reserved for the few, and participate joyfully in a true rebirth. A return to their legacy requires that we care for the Divine in the self and others through a living connection with our ancestors.

An African's expression of ancestral prayer
is celebrated not kneeling on a velvet cushion
in a stone building with stained glass windows on a
Sunday
but with sacred rituals and a dance
performed each night thanking the gods
for a life lived to the fullest
in spite of widespread spiritual genocide.

It is a dance of life performed
not on a multi-million dollar neon-lit stage
but in a circle of fire
under the watchful eye of the Moon and the Stars

with bodies robed not in fabrics made in foreign lands
but in those of our own design
and bare feet gently massaged by the sand.

It is a life dependent not on foreign aid
but anchored in the power of the invisible.
A life whose policies are drafted
by the United Angels of Afrika.

An African's prayer is a way of life
A return of humans to humanity
and humanity to humans.
Motho ke motho ka batho.

A wonderful thing about being in the business of soul construction is that every brick that you lay for another transforms itself into a mirror for you. As I help others to reflect on their lives, I see myself in them. One of the most difficult and often painful lessons that I have had to learn was to confront my dark side as reflected in others. Yet we will benefit from this kind of experience only when we learn to live our own truth.

What is my truth? What have I come here to do?
Who am I?

I am a sparrow that flies
High above the mountains
To listen to the messages of the wind.
Like a mermaid who sinks deep
Into the womb of the earth
To learn the teaching of the rocks.
Soaring like an eagle

Across the Afrikan lakes
To learn the language of the soul.
As I spread my wings with
The storm as my companion
I become one with my fear.
Who am I?
Some call me free spirit.

I am afraid. Yes, my truth does fill me with fear. However, it is when I learn to be one with my fear that it is suddenly transformed from a crippling force into nothing more than mild stage fright as I prepare to receive my legacy from the spirits of Onkgopotse Tiro, Sol Plaatjie, Robert Sobukwe and Joe Slovo. As I step forward, out of the corner of my eye I see the shadows of Pythagoras, Jan van Riebeeck, Cecil John Rhodes and Sir Winston Churchill leading a delegation from the West charged with the massive responsibility of giving back to Africa what belongs to her – her teachings, innovations, wealth and health.

I am going home
armed with a bosom full of
compassion and fierce tenacity
from the African Matriarchs
A calabash of wisdom
from the ancient healers residing in
the womb of Modimolle
Led by the guiding light of
Senakangwedi emanating from
the mouth of Limpopo
I am ready to come home.
Africa is my home.

Sistren connections

Just a week after I started writing this book, a very close friend and sister, Mado Keagile Modise, was killed in a horrible car accident. She was full of life; it was hard to let her die, and I grieved through the day and night. But somehow I felt that she would not be happy with all these tears. I knew that she would want me to let go. This letter helped me do just that – let her go home.

My dearest Keagile

A masterpiece indeed!! I am not sure if I am referring to you, or your dramatic exit, or both. My precious and beloved soul sister. How do I begin a dialogue with you now that you are formally formless? Girl, I knew that you could be unpredictable, but I never thought that you would outdo me on this one. Besides, our pact has always been that I go through something first and you follow. I'm the big sister, remember? So what made you think you could set a new trend?

I felt strangely euphoric when I got up yesterday, and the first thing I did was play some of my favourite jazz classics very loud – oldies like Johnny Hodges, Duke Ellington and Miles Davis. My music was so loud that Katlego asked which of us was the teenager in the house. I was over the moon, celebrating the current creative energy flowing through me endlessly and abundantly.

Just a week ago, when we spoke, you were complaining about my absence, about the fact that I spend so much time in Northern Province. Of course I miss you when I'm there, but don't you know that soul sisters stay connected in spite of the distance that separates them physically? Two days ago, when I told you about the book and joked about starting to write an international best-seller, you couldn't wait to read the manuscript. I had promised to read the poem for you too. I didn't want to send it by e-mail. I wanted to see the reaction on your face as I read it to you. But you weren't able to wait for either the poem or the book.

Well, I guess you had more urgent matters to attend to. You've always been one to attend to matters spontaneously, sometimes to your detriment. I relate to that part of you because I tend to be like that myself – an unguided missile, I've been called.

I am sitting here wondering how on earth I could have been so happy on the day of your exit. I guess that as a soul sister, I celebrated your spiritual release hours before it happened. Your take-off has stirred my latent yearning to learn to fly. Somehow, I refuse to accept that only birds and aeroplanes can fly. As you know, I have contemplated flying for some time now, but have been grounded by unfavourable weather conditions.

Mado, your take-off has given me fresh hope and the energy to live my life as determined by the Goddess. Your passing on has reinforced the lesson I have to learn about living each day to the fullest. Isn't it amazing that so many of us are knowledgeable, yet so few are wise?

I have to admit that I miss you, but I am happy for you. I will always remember you with tons of love and warmth. Do you remember a few weeks ago when we met on the highway on Sunday evening, driving home with our children after having spent the day with our respective parents? I remember the laughter, the hugs, the love, and the children. Do you remember Oratile and Kgalalelo laughing together, with Mothimane sleeping peacefully on Ousi's lap? You phoned me later to tell me about the fantastic jazz show on Metro. Ike Phaahla certainly put together an awesome collection that evening. Just for the two of us, we giggled. Laughter, your laughter, your funny way of telling jokes – that's how I'll remember you.

You and I have always been consciously grateful for our parents' love and care. We vowed never to take such blessings for granted. Now that you are gone, I will continue to keep that promise. I will spend as much time with my parents as I can; I will enjoy them to the fullest while they are still alive. I try to live my life in such a way that I have little or no room for regrets. Not that I haven't made my fair share of mistakes. After all, a life without mistakes is a life without expansion.

How I will miss our long e-mail exchanges, sometimes thoughtful and sometimes hilarious. Don't you dare get swollen headed, though, because you sent me a lot of junk too. But now we don't need any hardware or software – we have an exclusive and direct spiritual line.

I can never thank you enough for what we have shared. Laughter, tears, a carefree sparkle even when weighed down by the challenges that come disguised as problems. Do come and visit when your schedule is not too hectic. But knowing you, you'll probably end up volunteering to run all the errands.

Please, Mado, try not to worry about Oratile and Leruo; they will be raised with love. Remember, they are not your children, they merely came through you. You have raised them well. You are a good mother.

Go well my dear Sister; I love you with all my heart. And I know that you love me too.

O re tlogetse re sa solofela mmagwe batho
Re ntse re go tlhomile itlho kgomo
fa o budutsa lefatshe ka majato
e ka re o motho a sebelwa
ke tlhokwa la tsela.

Tshetsana ya mabono
sefatlhego e ka re o ne o
latswa ke nogakgolo
Matlho a gago kgogedi
malakabe a molelo o gotediwa
ke metlae le ditshegwana
jaaka dijo tsa gago tsa letsatsi.

Ka re o katogile monyo nnana
lethekana la mofu o ka re o kgosigadi
tsele la go ekete o amusa magosi le magosana
pelo ya go tswine re ka e rafa dinotshe
mowa o ela jaaka mashi a kgomo
e amusa lebotlana.
O re tlogetse re sa solofela mmagwe batho.

O re dumedisetse ko gae
Re kopele pholo ya mowa
ekete mowa wa gago o ka fetoga
metsi a nkgo ya mokgako
go re phekola malwetse mafaratlhatlha.

Mewa ya rona e solla le naga
e raletse melatswana le dithota
malapa a rona ke hube
le fa a sa tshwane le setlhe
re a nyelela, re tlhoka maitsetsepelo.

Lefatshe la borrarona le ela kgodu e khibidu
re garumana jaaka phologolo tsa naga
re kopele goboMmemogolo gore ba
re tlhatswetse marumo a bagale ba rona.
O re kopele thoti ya leokwane
go letefatsa maikutlo a a omileng
jaaka letlalo la mokoduwe wa mogoga.

O re tlogetse re sa solofela mmagwe batho
Re dumedisetse koo gae
Go fitlhela re kopana
Kgorong ya Badimo.

Till we meet again. Love you lots, always.
Mmatshilo

My roots

I come from a group of Batswana called *Bakgatla ba Mosetlha a Magana le Kgomo*. The home of the Bakgatla consists of a number of villages in the Moretele district ruled by *Kgosi* Makapan, with Mosetlha or Makapanstad as the head village. The village takes its name from the traditional ruler, *Kgosi* Seaparankwe Makapan.

Other villages around Mosetlha include Kgomo Kgomo, Radipapanne, Kontant, Moratele, Moretele, Tladistad, Dikebu, Mmatlhwaela, Bollantlokwe, Ramaratha, and Ngobi. My childhood memories consist of intact imprints of life in these villages. I am a descendant of the Bakgatla, *ba re a e namele setlhare e je borekhu namane ya kgabo*, and that makes me very proud.

Village life was simple and abundant. My people owned land, which they tilled to produce their own food. They owned cattle, and our earlier history contains no mention of malnutrition because the children were fed on unprocessed milk from our own herds. We did not depend on boxed cereals for nourishment; a maize cob was far more nutritious than a bowl of refined cereal served with diluted milk. We did not have to spend money on cream and butter from a supermarket owned by a white man; we made our own. We did not have to sell our labour in maize fields across the Highveld to earn money for food; we owned the fields. We never had to buy maize meal and so enrich the owners of milling companies; we ground our own.

The children had *dikgobe,* boiled corn and beans, as an in-between snack instead of *skopas,* the multi-coloured popcorn that today we so willingly buy in bulk from produce markets in the city to sell to our township children for 50 cents a packet. Apart from tasting like white bread soaked in sweet and sour water, that stuff is of no value to our bodies. Before we were bewitched by the white man, our bodies were temples that were fed with nothing but soul food. We did not require any white man's nutritional supplements, we did not have to depend on primary school feeding schemes; Mother Earth provided all in abundance.

All this did not fall as manna from heaven. Our ancestors worked hard, starting their day at dawn, tilling the land, milking the cows, grinding corn, taking good care of both their families and the environment. I still can't work out how we got to the point where we are today, when robust black men are confined to miniature prisons as they guard cluster homes in enclosed suburbs rather than following in the footsteps of their ancestors, who spent their days out in the open watching over their herds of cattle.

In those days, African time was not an hour or two after the designated time. African time was time on the dot, measured not by the smoothly rotating hands of a Rolex, but in terms of a life lived in harmony with the earth; *mahube a naka tsa kgomo, fa dikgomo di boela sakeng, ka sethoboloko, kgotsa fa dikgomo di ya go nwa metsi.* Unlike Western time, time in the villages was in harmony with the laws of nature and the environment. With the introduction of a watch, a relationship with the environment is lost. Time is no longer described in relation to events, but as an abstraction.

Whenever I arrange meetings with rural women, I am struck by their punctuality. On one never-to-be-forgotten occasion I was the only one with a car, a watch and a cell phone, yet I was the only one who was late. Equipped with all these modern gadgets meant to improve my sense of time and communication, I failed to honour their time. Instead, I arrived late, and found them all waiting in a circle under a tree. I realised then that African time is time on the dot; these women made sure that by the time I arrived, they were all waiting. This had meant leaving home long before the agreed time, not because they hadn't a car or a watch, but because they interpret time in relation to events. A meeting at eight o'clock in the morning will be associated with the time when local herdsmen leave the village with their cattle, or even with the time when children leave the house for school. Without depending on a watch or a car, my people were timeless, yet always on time.

My name is Mmatshilo, and I am named after an amazing woman, my paternal grandmother. The name "Mmatshilo" is derived from the stone used by my people to grind corn. I am the mother (Mma) of the stone (tshilo). My name has been appropriate to the various phases of my evolution as a woman. Those who have known me from my earliest childhood call me "Ntshilo". A few of my crazy childhood friends used to call me "Ntyilo Ntyilo", taken from a classic South African jazz tune played by artists such as Winston Mankunku Ngozi. In my earlier years as a gender activist, I unleashed significant amounts of anger and bitterness on the world because of the psychological wounds I had suffered, and at that time "Mmatshilo" embodied a grinding force and all the other qualities often identified by capitalist

27

societies as being desirable for growth, although their potential to destroy the soul is never mentioned. More recently, as I matured into a woman fallen completely in love with herself, "Mmatshilo" became the one who grinds corn, thereby nourishing herself and others. I love my name for its sheer versatility; it fits all that I have been, all that I am.

I am also named after my father's aunt, Ntswatswa, born of Motsei and married into the Kiletji family. My father tells of the debate that ensued when I was born, with elders arguing that I could not be named after two old women because I might turn out to be mad.

I come from an interesting line of ancestors. My mother, Boitumelo Tladi, is the daughter of Mamoabi Herminah Setshedi and Ramatlhodi Hoffen Tladi. My grandfather, Ramatlhodi, was born in Makapanstad and later purchased land and property in Lady Selbourne in the 1930s, where he lived until his untimely death in 1946. It was a sudden death; he was killed by *ga le phirime*, which means "the sun will not set". According to my mother, witchcraft was rife at the time and people used all kinds of potions to maim and kill. One such potion was commonly put in beer. Once consumed it proved lethal in less than 24 hours, hence its name.

During his lifetime, my grandfather was a land and property owner. There are many like him, recorded and unrecorded. From Winterveldt to Lady Selbourne, Alexandra to Evaton, Sophiatown to District Six, our people had their names inscribed on title deeds as rightful and proud property owners who contributed to the economy of the country. Now, because of well-known historical acts of theft and fraud, many are landless and homeless. Instead of having been adequately reimbursed, they are now perceived as a liability, responsible for the declining value of property or the state of the environment.

The sensitivity of the land question is as deep as our national wound. Opting for convenient amnesia in our attempts to heal this wound will have the same effect as covering an abscess with a sticking plaster. Without an incision to drain the wound and the application of a disinfectant, the dis-ease-causing organisms will multiply, spreading the infection beyond the initial locus. We cannot afford the luxury of paralysed liberal thinking. We have to overcome our paralysis and begin to act in the way that deep down we know to be right.

My grandmother, Mamoabi Herminah Setshedi, was born in Makapanstad in 1894. My mother, too, was born in Makapanstad, and when she was very young moved with my grandparents to Lady Selbourne, where the family lived at 394 Alexander Street, on the corner of Alexander and Achilles. My grandmother was a domestic worker. She died of a stroke at 73 in a taxi on her way to work in Pretoria West. I grieve for the fact that our grandparents never had the time, nor the luxury of retirement policies, for retirement and rest. Yet many, like my grandmother, loved their work and derived a sense of pride from working until their last day on earth. African people lazy?

The perception of Africans as lazy people is nothing but a fabrication. Our men have sweated blood building the wealth of the country; our women have tirelessly kept the African home fires burning in their husbands' absence. Yet in spite of giving our all, our balance sheets still record a material and spiritual deficit. Is it because of this deficit that we have come to internalise the blatant lie that Africans are lazy?

Like many women of earlier generations who grew up in Africa, my grandmother's day started at three o'clock in the morning, when she got up to make the fire and prepare hot water for the family before she herself went to work to take good care of a white madam's home and children. Even when my mother was a nurse at the HF Verwoerd Hospital, my grandmother still woke early to make sure that my mother had had tea by the time she left to catch what the locals called a Kalamazoo bus at four in the morning. The bus ride from Lady Selbourne to Pretoria cost a tickey, the equivalent of two and a half cents today.

My grandmother was a devout Christian, and forbade us to play the gramophone on Sundays. She had simple tastes, and was down to earth and rooted as a black woman. She left instructions that when she died, her funeral was to be very simple, and that she was to be buried in an inexpensive coffin. On the day of her funeral, the undertakers struggled repeatedly and unsuccessfully to lower her body into the grave. As this was happening, my mother noticed the green mats that undertakers often put around graves, and she remembered her mother asking for a very simple funeral. My mother whispered to the undertakers to remove the mats, and my grandmother was lowered to her final resting place with ease. I wonder what she would have to say about the current practice of expensive funerals, designer suits and sunglasses, cell phones ringing at the graveside, and after-tears parties.

My grandmother was blessed with five children, my four uncles, Pheko, Boy, Mpoko and Rankakata (affectionately known by everyone, children and adults alike, as Bra Nick), and my mother. Of all my uncles, I was closest to Bra Nick. Nick Tladi was a charismatic man who never allowed life to get him down. He was a comedian even when facing life's toughest and most horrendous lessons. At his funeral, mourners were laughing as people narrated some of the things that he used to say or do. He was indeed given a joyful send-off. However, I am still sad that he left us so early in life. There was so much to learn from him, and this book would have been richer had he still been alive.

Like most black men of the time, he started his career as a teacher. He then went on to become one of the first radio announcers for Radio Bantu, together with the likes of Nick Thabo Mokwena, Justice Tshungu, Dan Setshedi and Getz Komane. In those days, the radio waves were in the hands of mature men, most of them teachers. Today most radio stations have turned commercial, focusing on generating revenue as opposed to facilitating an in-depth and intensive psychological re-orientation and education in response to pertinent societal challenges. Nowadays our ears and minds are fed an exclusive diet of American music, with the exception of one week in the year dubbed "South African music week". That we should allocate just one of the fifty-two weeks of the year to a celebration of ourselves speaks volumes.

I spent some of my school holidays visiting Bra Nick and his family, first in Atteridgeville, where they lived with my maternal grandmother, and later in Ga Rankuwa in four-roomed homes in Zones 16 and 4 next to Uncle Nat's and Sakie's Dry Cleaners respectively. Those little matchbox houses have such stories to tell, testimony to the injustice of the indigenous majority being allocated a mere 13 per cent of the land. Yet they are testimony to something else too. Tenacity. Those houses were meant to dehumanise, but those who lived in them made the best of the substandard living conditions. Our mothers prided themselves on creating flourishing flower and vegetable gardens, producing the most memorable carrots, tomatoes, spinach – and beetroot, of course. No special township meal is complete without beetroot. It was from our yards that we enjoyed fruit such as peaches, grapes and mulberries, and our mothers bottled peaches and made mulberry jam, which we enjoyed either with bread for breakfast, or over our porridge for dinner.

In those days, in the 1970s and 80s, it was common to see boys and girls on their knees polishing the stoep with red Sunbeam polish, or sweeping the entire yard, including the area outside the gate. We lived in a ghetto, yet we possessed abundant self-pride, reflected in the cleanliness and beauty of our environment in spite of our poor living conditions. Before the construction of beer halls and overflowing wells of Chibuku in our communities, making our men slaves to alcohol, family and communal life was the pride of our existence. Care for the self through caring for others and the environment has always been part of our make-up.

Because historically our people practised totemism, we revered animals and plants. For example, the Bakgatla associate themselves with the monkey, the Bakwena with the crocodile, the Batlhaping with the fish. Identification with a particular animal means that those who associate themselves with that animal can neither kill it nor kill other life forms on which its life depends. So, if you were a Mokgatla, you would be discouraged from senselessly cutting down trees, because the monkey loves trees, a Motlhaping would not dream of polluting the river because the fish depends on unpolluted water to survive, and so on.

To connect with their ancestors, my foreparents said their prayers around *legwama*, a special plant grown in every homestead. Our ancient history is pregnant with stories relating to the reciprocal connection between people and their environment. Our ancestors were prayerful and contemplative ecological practitioners. Sadly, we have, over time, unquestioningly embraced the teachings of the missionaries, and under their tutelage we have come to attack the teachings of our ancestors, rejecting our connection with them as being pagan or even demonic, and exchanging our heritage for Sunday churchgoing and Bible reading. We have, over the years, taken a significant amount of psychological battering. The state of our environment is testimony to our internal hurts. All the litter that we see with our physical eyes is a symptom of a deep emotional and spiritual wound. Our soul is broken. Our sense of pride has been torn into pieces, to be blown against barbed wire fences by subtle yet powerful winds. I do not advocate embracing a psychology of victimhood, yet I feel that it is time to acknowledge and confront our wounds at a personal, family and community level, and to take the advice of the eminent African American woman writer bell hooks, who encourages us to reclaim our triumph and pain without shame.

Our liberation has cost us a whole lot more than we are willing to admit. It is time to accept that we have been wounded and that we need healing, time to introduce our values of being one with the earth as embodied in African healing practices into Western psychology and environmental work. It is time to reframe environmental conservation as part of our agenda for healing. Healing and cleansing the environment is not the exclusive preserve of Western practitioners. Before being enslaved by money and consumerism, traditional healers were guided by specific principles in their interaction with the environment. There were certain seasons designated for harvesting herbs. There were also specific ways of harvesting herbs without destroying the ecosystem. Where fresh plant material was needed, a healer harvested only the amount needed, as opposed to the current practice of hoarding entire plants and animals for sale.

Discussions with elders in the villages reveal that caring for the environment was a spiritual practice. Humanity was viewed as interdependent with all other life forms. Because of their total dependence on the environment, traditional communities lived their lives in ways that encouraged harmony and balance with the earth, water, animals, plants and the entire universe. With their reverence for life in all its forms, these communities viewed the health of each individual as inextricably bound up with the health of the planet. This explains why seeking refuge in the woods or on top of a mountain overlooking a mighty river is acknowledged as one of the ancient paths to awakening to Mother Earth.

All this means that clean-up campaigns in our communities will remain fruitless if they fail to incorporate mechanisms not only for establishing economic self-reliance that preserves our culture and our environment, but also for healing the soul. Our future cannot, must not, depend on foreign investments whose ultimate outcomes include destroying our moral and cultural fibre by building "lost cities" in our precious ecosystems and villages. There is so much more to the life of an African than total dependence on a foreigner whose wealth and wisdom may well have been acquired through theft and fraud. That we continue to depend on the proceeds of global criminality for the reclamation of our being is beyond me.

As I mentioned, my mother was born in Makapanstad, but moved to Lady Selbourne when she was still little, making her, like so many of us, an urban girl of rural origins. I spent my childhood in a number of rural villages, interspersed with periods in the township: my family on my mother's side is primarily urbanised, while my family on my father's side has very strong rural roots. This explains why I still divide my time between Johannesburg and the dusty and sunny village of Kgomo Kgomo and its surrounds.

During their school holidays, my children visit their grandparents, and embrace the challenge of playing and communicating without using a single word of English. Seeing my daughter, Kgalalelo, participating in and enjoying the same indigenous games that I played as a girl makes me happy. Seeing her running around, shouting and laughing with her peers without missing her computer or television, is an amazing experience. Instead of going to sleep-over parties, movies or hanging out in the malls, my teenage son, Katlego, spends time with his grandfather looking after the cattle, repairing the windmill to provide drinking water for the animals, fixing the fence or learning to drive the tractor. Watching my youngest son, Onkgopotse, playing in sand not confined to a sandpit is an absolute delight. Without the luxury of toys, surrounded by chickens, goats and puppies, my son's horizons open up. I so hope that spending time in both an urban and a rural environment will give my children a balanced view of life. There is so much more to life than an addiction to technological gadgets and the trap of consumerism.

The fact that my mother was raised amongst four robust boys probably explains why she is so vocal and outspoken. She is a woman of boundless energy and zest for life, and completely fits the saying *"Mmangwana o tshwara thipa ka fa bogaleng"*. She occupies her space powerfully, and I can see why my father was attracted to her and later chose her to raise his children.

As I say this, however, I wonder about the extent to which she was influenced by the common view of a mother as a strong woman. Now that I am an adult woman myself, I know that as a woman she has experienced pain. While I have no memory of her in a state of fear or panic, I know that there were times when she was afraid. As someone who is consulted by a multitude of people who are going through life's challenges, I can't help wondering: does she have somewhere to go when she feels overwhelmed? She is a selfless and giving woman, but she is human too. As children, we expect our mothers to cope for our sake. Society is not structured in a way that supports mothers who may break down, either permanently or temporarily, when the pain and suffering become unbearable. Mothers know just how heavy the burden of "being a good mother" under very difficult circumstances can be. Some mothers don't make it, and turn to alcohol and other addictions, suffer psychosomatic illnesses and ultimately take their own lives. Indeed, many mothers have died in pain and distress. They all did the very best they could. May their Souls rest in peace.

At this point in my life, my mother and I have become the greatest of friends. I have rediscovered myself as a woman in my relationship with my mother – talk about a cycle of nourishing womanist healing energy! I am who I am because of having enjoyed the warmth of her womb and nourishment from her physical breasts. I continue to grow in leaps and bounds because of the strength I draw from her spiritual breast.

In many ways, an honest and loving relationship with one's mother is crucial for the health of the earth. Have you ever thought deeply about the name "Mother Earth"? Have you considered why Vusi Mahlasela composed the song "The earth I know is a woman"? Did Jimmy Dludlu perhaps take his inspiration from Mother Earth when he penned "Motherland", which happens to be one of my all-time favourite tunes (and he my favourite artist)? What do you think was Paul Hanmer's inspiration when he put together "Meeting of the women"? Can you conceive of what the atmosphere in the studio must have been like during the recording of this powerful song, pregnant with feminine energy? This is the time for a collective healing of a wounded womanhood; it is time to heal and nurture the relationship between mothers and their daughters. This is the moment in our evolution for mothers and daughters to speak honestly, truthfully, openly and lovingly. Only then can we reclaim and embrace both our womanhood and femininity in a world that has been largely defined by manhood and masculinity.

It is time to return to Mother Earth. However, a return to Mother Earth is not a pilgrimage exclusively for women. The time also calls for men to embrace their positive feminine and masculine energy. I hear many leading black men speak with the utmost respect and compassion about their mothers, yet sadly I find that this reverence for black womanhood does not apply to other black women in their lives, such as their wives and girlfriends. Similarly, I have witnessed a great number of black women using their masculine energy in collaborating with the erosion of the black male psyche. This is something I myself have been guilty of. Yet the truth is that we can no longer support a revolution that makes others or ourselves vulnerable and invisible. It is time to heal.

Our healing as a nation requires that we go beyond breaking the chains of racial oppression. We must also eradicate the negative effects of patriarchy and sexism on our individual and collective psyche. To live harmoniously as women and men, we must nurture both the intuitive feminine and action-oriented masculine to create a balanced union. It is indeed the time for the sacred integration of the feminine and masculine.

From girl child to womanhood

I was born at Holy Cross Nursing Home in Lady Selbourne in November 1959. My date of birth makes me a Sagittarian, rough edges and all. I have never really been a firm believer in horoscopes, except when the predictions revealed what I wanted to hear. Any comments on my shadow side or anything negative I quickly gloss over as not being meant for me, but for another Sagittarian living under different planetary influences, and probably in another part of the world!

My evolution as a woman born and living in Africa has been influenced by so many factors that I cannot even begin to capture them in a single publication. While many are visible and can be experienced consciously, some are abstract and invisible. Wailing for the first time outside my mother's womb, little did I know that *Baas* Verwoerd had a few years earlier passed legislation intended to make me "a hewer of wood and a drawer of water" and to prevent me from discovering my essence or determining my own destiny.

I attended pre-school in Lady Selbourne and Atteridgeville in Pretoria as well as Makapanstad in Hammanskraal. This sort of perpetual motion was the lot of all black families, moved about at random as the result of a host of socio-economic and political factors. My father, who was a civil servant, a Bantu school board secretary, to be precise, was always faced with the possibility of a transfer from one place to another. I have never managed to figure out the selection criteria used by the *groot baas* in those days to decide on a promotion, which invariably translated into a transfer. In most instances, promotion meant that the employee had to leave at short notice, and without his family.

It's true what they say about there being many ways to skin a cat. While the majority of black working class men were herded into overcrowded, single-sex hostels, a significant number considered educated were sentenced to the solitary occupation of decent houses in isolated postings far away from their support base. Irrespective of whether the worker had to wear overalls and search for gold underground using *fanakalo* to communicate or whether he wore a tie and worked in an office typing letters in the King's English on an old typewriter, the effects were the same. That system killed the root of our society, our families.

Following my rollercoaster pre-school years with a stint at a crèche run by Staff Nurse Mosaka at Makapanstad Clinic, I started my first year of school at the Lutheran Church at the age of five. At the beginning of the year I had no-one to care for me at home, as my parents went to work. They asked Mistress Thibedi to do so for a while. Of necessity, I had to spend some time in her classroom – one month turned into twelve, and at the end of the year I had not merely passed, but passed very well.

This is one part of my life story I love narrating. My children have heard many different versions of the story (adults never lie!) and have even threatened voluntary exile if the story is inflicted on them again. But it involves defying the odds, and so I am happy to tell it again. At the time, a five-year-old black girl child in a remote village was never regarded as being ready for school. Many were forced to wait until after they turned seven or sometimes even later. Historically, school readiness has been enormously controversial because it has been racially biased. The journey that this five-year-old girl embarked on from the Lutheran Church in Makapanstad to Senteng and Bahwaduba Primary Schools in Mathibestad was an interesting one. I drive through that area a lot on my way to Kgomo Kgomo and Dikebu. Seeing young children walking along the same paths I used to and from school warms my soul. In my heart of hearts I know that even though they look deprived, they can and will defy the odds and make history in one way or another.

Driving through the area also stirs up memories of some of the teachers who made an indelible mark on my life. The first, of course, is Mistress Thibedi, or Ma-Thibedi, as we affectionately called her. However, I have noticed with concern that male teachers dominate my school memories. We live in a society that does not value women's work, especially the work done by our mothers, and our pre-school and junior primary teachers, most of whom are women.

My teachers at Bahwaduba Higher Primary School include Teacher Tabane (who has now passed on), and the energetic and vibrant Teacher Phalatse, who played a significant role in encouraging me to strive for the best. After I had been in his standard five class for three months, he promoted me to standard six. I went home delighted, to report this news to my father. At the time, my mother was away for a year, studying for a diploma in public health at Ga Rankuwa Hospital. My father took full responsibility for the children in my mother's absence, and he has had a powerful influence on my life. He always insisted that his girls should get an education because of the hardships that women in particular have to face in life.

As the eldest child in a family of five, I think I encountered the wrath of the rod more than any of my siblings. My father meted out most of the physical punishment. While discipline is the responsibility of both parents, physical discipline seems to be reserved for fathers, with mothers threatening to report their children's sins of omission or commission to their fathers on their return from work. Many men reinforce the image of "the one to be feared", to the extent that when father comes home children scatter, pretending to be busy while dad enjoys watching television alone or reading the paper. By doing that, most fathers miss out on a much deeper level of psychological bonding with their children. Watching my father now and knowing what a deeply sensitive man he is, I wonder whether he truly believed in beating us, or whether he was merely acting out what he had been taught. I have seen him in situations when he needed to cry, but, being a man, could not. Something amazing about him, though, is that whenever he needed to cry but could not, he always expressed his feelings in words. As a woman who has witnessed powerful glimpses of her feminine, I fully understand how he feels when he experiences a need to express a deep emotion, yet feels incapable of doing so because the action would be perceived as being inappropriate for his gender. This only makes me love him more. Within a range of financial, political and cultural constraints, he has done his best to prepare me for life.

My father has met so many more than just my economic needs. He is a man of few words, yet he communicates in his silence. I have warm memories of his support during the most difficult times of my life. He would, on occasion, drive from Kgomo Kgomo to be with my children and me at my Johannesburg home. Without saying much, he would spend the evening with us, sometimes even sleeping on the couch as we watched television. After spending the night, he would set out very early for home the next morning. My father has never expressed his love in words, but I have never doubted its presence. He was there whenever I received a prize or award at school. He taught me to drive at thirteen. He was a fast driver, and I have obviously turned out to be like him. At one time I accumulated so many speeding fines and had so many heated exchanges with traffic officers between Ga Rankuwa and Mabopane that they even went to report my behaviour to him. We were living in Mabopane at the time, and he was a senior government official at Odi Magistrate's Court in Ga Rankuwa. He cautioned me about my driving, at which I couldn't help thinking, "But you taught me to drive!"

In spite of his meagre salary first as a teacher in Tladistad, then as a Bantu school board secretary in the Makapanstad circuit office, after which he occupied administrative positions in various government offices, my father occasionally treated his family to a holiday away from home. The first time we went to Durban we travelled in a battered Toyota Hilux, with logs and sheets of plastic as a makeshift canopy. I remember how cold we children were in the back, arguing over blankets and whether the sun in fact rose from the west, as my cousin Charlie claimed, as we drove through Harrismith in the

Free State. We were completely disoriented after having left our home at three o'clock in the morning. But all the discomfort was forgotten the moment we saw the ocean for the very first time.

My father was used to driving long distances, often leaving home in the early hours of the morning. Just like my father, I spend a lot of my time on the road, and like him I start early, with *Mphatlalatsane*, the morning star, above me and the cool breeze across my face. Watching the sun rise from the darkness while driving across a beautiful landscape is a truly uplifting experience. My most memorable sunrise took place one Sunday. I was in the open veld with my father and my sons, with a small stone from my grandfather's grave in the palm of my hand, giving offerings to the gods. As the sun emerged, the moon was about to sink away after a night of giving silver light. There was I, a modern yet traditional African woman who was simultaneously a granddaughter, a daughter and a mother, surrounded by the men in my life and connecting with my male ancestral spirits. From Sun the God and Moon the Goddess I received the teaching that a marriage between a self-loving masculine and self-affirming feminine gives birth to Stars that shine brightest in the darkest hour.

But to return to my school days. How can I ever forget that whirlwind of a man, Teacher Molamu? I remember those long legs ending in feet encased in a pair of black Grasshoppers, and the fact that he constantly hummed a tune as he flew along the school corridors like a tornado. He loved choral music. Teacher Phalatse loved music too, and was one of the best conductors. One thing that I disliked, though, was being made to sing individually during choir practice, as the shortcomings of those of us who lacked the golden voice of a MaBrr were exposed – and no amount of cod liver oil or Sen Sens ever worked any magical transformation on my vocal cords.

Nevertheless, I loved participating in regional music competitions. Together with soccer and netball, choral music competitions created opportunities for us to travel in a bus and get to see new places. These were not our only extra-curricular activities, though: we also experienced the 'joys' of cleaning the windows, sweeping classrooms and the schoolyard with brooms made of grass (and inhaling a lot of dust in consequence), and of fetching water for the vegetable garden and weeding the schoolyard in the scorching sun.

On some occasions, when the girls were cleaning the classrooms and windows, boys could be heard playing soccer on the playing field. Not happy with this injustice, some of the more athletic girls would storm the soccer field, grab the ball and run to an area adjacent to the staff room. As expected, the boys would set off in pursuit, causing a commotion that called for a teacher's intervention. After heated debate, the teacher would instruct the boys to help with moving furniture in the classroom.

I spent most of my time in the boys' company, but after such an event, I would find myself without a companion on the way home from school. This never lasted too long, though. In a matter of days, the boys and I would be back in trouble for hanging on to the back of the coal truck and screaming "*Boramalatlha*" at the driver and deliverymen.

During one of these death-defying escapades one of the men lashed out and hit me on the head, causing a gaping wound. When my father asked what had happened, I replied, "I fell". My father was rightly disbelieving, and the truth was finally forced out of my mouth with a lashing. Once I told the truth, I thought the beating would stop, but I was lashed first for not telling the truth, and then for riding at the back of the truck, yelling at men who were old enough to be my father, and for getting myself hurt.

On another occasion I fell out of a tree and broke my collarbone. This happened during school holidays, when I was in Kgomo Kgomo visiting my grandparents. I spent my days climbing trees with the boys, catching insects called *mamtinti*, and piercing their abdomens with a thorn, which made them produce a strange sound when they flew. On this particular day, I was at the top of the tree with Motjile, a distant cousin who gave himself the name Drinking Tea to show off his knowledge of English. I was right at the top, reaching out to catch an insect on an adjacent branch, when I lost my balance and fell, hitting the ground hard. For one very long second I lay there, numbed and petrified. My cousin Drinking Tea sensed the storm that would follow, and disappeared into thin air.

My grandmother was furious, and sent someone to call *Mmamogolo* from her house next door. They took me inside and sent someone to inform my father in Makapanstad. My parents arrived some time later and, not unexpectedly, my father wanted to give me a hiding. Through the grace of the Lord and my mother's intervention, the rod was miraculously spared, but with promises of what I would receive in the way of punishment once I was discharged from hospital.

I was admitted to Jubilee Hospital in Hammanskraal for two weeks. I cannot remember if they had children's wards at the time, because I was admitted to an overcrowded adult female ward, where I had to share a bed with another woman, and sleep at the foot of the bed. Those two weeks were boring, and the only thing to look forward to was my parents' daily visits, as they often brought delicacies that I didn't regularly get at home.

In spite of hating my stay in hospital and having to endure being kicked by the woman whose bed I shared while she slept (I still remember her cracked heels), I did not want to be discharged. The thought of my father carrying out his promise was enough to make me consider asking the doctor to declare my injuries terminal. When the day did eventually come, my parents drove me home and my father broke his promise. I never got the lashing. While I would normally view the breaking of a promise in a serious light, on that occasion my father's omission received my undivided support and blessings.

Another of my memories of Teacher Phalatse involves the time he caught me and the boys gambling, playing *kap kap* one afternoon not very far from school. He gave us a very stern warning, and the instruction to report to his office the next day. This was good news for me. As the only girl amongst the guilty due for prosecution, I could wear my thick bloomers stuffed with rags to reduce the pain of the teacher's cane. The next day, lined up with the boys, I received just as many lashes as they did. Gender equality indeed!

I remember Teacher Molefe and Teacher Thema who taught me Setswana and English at Hebron High School. Teacher Thema encouraged me to write and to participate in the debating team, which I enjoyed a great deal, particularly when we debated the famous topic

"The hand that rocks the cradle rules the world". I thoroughly enjoyed taking my male opponents through their paces! Teacher Molefe loved Setswana, the language of my ancestors, and was proud to explain to us the origins of common sayings (*dikapuo*) and proverbs (*diane*), which make African languages so rich. Dramatic, roundabout and full of humour, African languages were made to communicate. With African people being so animated, a normal conversation can very easily be mistaken for a theatre performance, staged against the backdrop of a taxi rank or local market.

I remember, too, Messrs Fourie and Meyer, who taught me Mathematics and Physics at Hebron. Mr Meyer was very old, so old that I wondered why he was still teaching. He had a hearing problem so we had to raise our voices when speaking to him, while he, in turn, was barely audible, and we could hardly make out whether the lesson was in English or Afrikaans or both. I remember him in constant conversation with himself in his periodic walkabouts around the school premises.

I have to confess that even though I passed Higher Grade maths and science, I never enjoyed them. It is only as an adult that I realise that had I been exposed to the arts early in my schooling, I would definitely have pursued a career in that direction. I am most concerned about the current overemphasis on mathematics, science and technology, and a decline in the appreciation for the role of indigenous languages and African artistic expression in our education system. We run the risk of producing engineers and information specialists who have no clue about who they are or what life is all about. Is it a good thing to focus on increasing the number of doctors from previously disadvantaged communities, yet ignore the importance of incorporating African values and healing systems in their training? Should we be satisfied with producing excellent heart surgeons who can neither communicate with their patients nor be bothered about the socio-cultural factors resulting in the sudden increase in the number of black men dying of heart attacks? It this the price to pay for civilisation? In the words of Credo Mutwa: "The only thing that can save us is to tell the foreigners openly that we do not wish to have their alien creeds, dogmas, beliefs and philosophies rammed down our throats. The sons of Africa must let the world know that we can well do without civilisation if this means that we have to throw our own culture, beliefs and way of life overboard".[1]

We have willingly handed over our children to private schools to be intellectually moulded by white teachers who speak a foreign language and follow a curriculum that is reluctant to draw from the values and ancient teachings of Africa. Our very own children call adult men and women working in their school grounds as cleaners and gardeners by their first names. Once I overheard my daughter referring to the old man selling ice cream on the school premises as "Frans". "Would you refer to *Ntatemogolo* as 'John'?" I asked her. (My father's first name is John.) When my daughter replied that she would not, because that would be disrespectful, I asked whether *Ntate* Frans (who is almost the same age as her grandfather) did not deserve the same respect. Even though our children may speak English, using the respectful *Ntate, Ntatemogolo, Mme* and *Koko* ought to be part of their vocabulary when communicating with our elders. It makes no difference whether the person happens to be a grandparent, a school gardener or a driver who picks them up from school.

[1] Mutwa, C. 1998. *Indaba, My Children: African Tribal History, Legends, Customs and Religious Beliefs*. Edinburgh: Payback Press: p.692.

I remember listening to a radio discussion on the role of African languages in contemporary society, and hearing a parent say that our languages are useless and that we should encourage our children to speak English because it is the language of business. Increasingly, anyone who majors in Setswana, isiZulu, TshiVenda or any other African language is considered unemployable. And this in a country where the majority of the people hardly speak English. Would a student who majored in Portuguese be treated that way in Portugal? I visited Ireland some years ago, and learnt that the Irish are re-learning their language via the medium of radio after having lost Irish to English. I remember thinking at the time that South Africans would soon be in the same position. In spite of being in the majority, we may well lose our languages, and we need to do something about it before it's too late.

During the school holidays, we visited my paternal grandmother, Mmatshilo. She used to wake us at dawn to fetch water from a pump located quite a distance from home, near to Nokanapedi, a river running between Kontant and Kgomo Kgomo. We slept in the same room as my grandmother, she on her bed and we children on the floor. When it was cold, though, she allowed us on to her bed to share the warmth of a hot water bottle or a steel iron wrapped in an old towel. She woke us every morning between half past four and five o'clock by calling *"Metlapa, tsogang ke motshegare"* – "Come on, lazybones, can't you see it's daybreak?" My sister, Lenyalo always pulled the curtain aside to check whether this was in fact true, and of course, every time she checked, she was greeted by inky darkness. My cousin, Mokou, always had trouble getting out of bed. She has very big eyes and I remember her walking around with those eyes half closed, and granny wanting to know whether she was awake or sleepwalking.

Even though we hated waking so early, it saved us from spending the whole morning in the heat waiting for our turn to get water. On the rare occasions that we overslept (which didn't happen often, as granny seemed to be equipped with an internal alarm clock), on our arrival at the pump, we would be greeted by a long and winding line of containers waiting for their turn to be filled. To while away the time, we played *diketo, morabaraba, kgati* or *mpatla* – all indigenous games played outdoors and involving group effort; through our play we acquired people skills and learnt values such as co-operation and teamwork. While games such as *kgati* required physical agility, others, such as *diketo* and *morabaraba*, improved our physical and mental co-ordination. These games stand in stark contrast to the violent computer games and pornographic material that have become easily accessible to today's children, who spend their time at home in voluntary solitary confinement with a "do not disturb" sign on their closed bedroom door.

When we returned from fetching the water, granny allocated chores – sweeping the yard, making the fire, and preparing our breakfast of porridge, tea and *dikromola*, dried slices of bread that my aunt, who was a domestic worker, sent regularly from Johannesburg. In spite of granny's early training, household chores have failed to make it to the top of my priority list. Even then I preferred settling in a corner with a book rather than cooking, cleaning, and ironing, and I often got into trouble with granny for disappearing with a book before finishing my duties. I love books and bookstores to this day; my fondness for them is perhaps rivalled only by my love of music. My father introduced me to jazz in my teens, and used to take me to jam sessions at the American Embassy building in Pretoria. I also clearly remember one of my cousins, Mantsho (affectionately known as "The Black"), playing jazz records on the gramophone with his friends, enjoying a beer together after polishing their Florsheim shoes. Those pointed shoes with their everlasting shine were just meant for dancing to jazz music. Yes, music truly is food for the soul.

After completing my basic nursing training I started work as a registered nurse at Ga Rankuwa Hospital, I spent my first pay cheque on a music system. My mother was torn between horror and amusement. Women buy household goods with their first pay, and what did I buy – a Sansui and LPs from Kohinoor Records! But that's my philosophy: let me first feed my soul. The plates, pots and spoons can come later.

From what I've been told, food for the soul has been more important to me than food for the body ever since babyhood, as my mother's attempts to get me to eat were completely unsuccessful. Since childhood I have been eating to live rather than living to eat, which means that treating me to an intimate three-course dinner by candlelight in an exquisite restaurant would not necessarily be a wise investment. I would much rather have a home-cooked meal in the company of very loud friends and family all talking at the same time – that way, my inability to finish all the food on my plate may go unnoticed.

I am, however, learning to appreciate food. My favourite meals include sour porridge with pumpkin leaves and ground peanuts, butternut soup with olive bread, grilled prawns, and samp and beans. I adore yellow peppers; their colour is divine. Eggplants also tend to find their way into my basket a lot these days during my visits to the market. I have come to the conclusion that cooks are artists; the kitchen is their studio and the dining room their gallery. I am fascinated by the process of mixing ingredients of different shapes, textures and colours, ending with a delightful product. I enjoy cooking up a storm for a troop of ravenous children and male siblings, but on one condition: that I cut vegetables while jamming to Bob Marley or some other musician-cum-magician. I love the combination of the intoxicating energy from the CD and the pattering of my children's bare feet as they run in and out of the kitchen.

As far as relationships and sex are concerned, I was a late bloomer. I guess it was because I was always in the company of boys – even felt that I could have been a boy – that I never felt any pressure to be under them to win their attention. Besides, I beat some of them physically during our after-school bouts. As the first child, I didn't have any brothers to watch over me, and I had to learn to defend myself. To tell the truth though, I relied more on my speed than my punch. For a hundred metres sprinter, flight felt much more natural than fight.

Overall, I was happy with who I was. I felt good enough and whole. Actually, many boys were petrified of approaching me to declare their love to me. I have lived with men's fear in this department right up to adulthood. I won't lie and pretend that that never bothered me – it did bother me at one point in my life, but not any more. Now I feel that anyone who is scared of me or threatened by me in any way will never be able to enjoy me fully.

To some extent, I have also used men's fears for my own empowerment. As a woman growing up, I learnt to make the first move myself rather than wait for a man. I had the feeling that if I waited, I was going to be waiting a very long time. That men can be such cowards is an open secret. Why and how society decided to award them the sole responsibility of initiating relationships and business deals and negotiating political settlements remains a mystery.

Looking back on that part of my life, though, and considering the woman I am today, I have to confess that I sometimes wonder whether there wasn't a little extra testosterone in my system then. Maybe that's the imbalance responsible for some of my life's significant discomforts and lessons. I am not complaining. I am my life story. And I am grateful for all my experiences and all my teachers, and my mother especially, for their support on my journey towards a reclamation of my femininity, the discovery of a balance between my feminine and masculine energies.

In my evolution as a woman, I have received many lessons, and there is one that I would like to share here because it is relevant to all women. Like most women, I hated menstruation and was forever looking for ways of manipulating my natural cycle. Practising as a nurse, I never understood why women consulted the doctor because they had not been to the Moon for many months. Essentially, all they were asking the doctor for was help to go to the Moon again. I never understood why they wanted to fix something that was, according to me, not broken. As a young woman, I suffered from menstrual cramps and was told that the condition would improve following the birth of my children. I have given birth to three children, but did not experience any relief until recently. Aside from having painful periods, like many women, I suffered from pre-menstrual syndrome, or PMS. That, combined with my natural fire energy, meant that anything could happen at that time of the month.

A lot of research has been done on PMS over the years. While many see it as a purely physiological phenomenon, emerging research shows that unresolved emotional problems, childhood trauma and high levels of stress could also have a role to play in the prevalence and severity of PMS. More than half of all women suffer from PMS from adolescence through to their thirties and forties.

There are several explanations for this. Women in their thirties and forties undergo a process of individuation and a letting go of some of the messages they internalised while growing up as girls in a culture that tends to view anything that is exclusively female as inferior, unclean or evil. Confirming the belief that a woman is dirty or evil, there are certain times in her life that society regards her as untouchable – widowhood, while she is menstruating, and a period after abortion, for example. In interviews with women elders in some of the villages, I learnt that they believe that the high prevalence of death amongst young men is attributable not only to Aids-related illnesses, but poisoning caused by sleeping with women who are menstruating. The notion of woman as unclean ties up with the fact that sexually transmitted infections are commonly referred to as women's diseases.

In addition to this negativity, women in contemporary society also face increasing levels of sexual violence, the breaking down of relationships and the challenges posed by trying to find a balance between a career and motherhood. The dilemma is further compounded by living in a society obsessed with competition, measurable outputs and economic growth. These circumstances virtually guarantee unresolved emotional conflict and trauma. After all, how can a woman possibly focus on her screaming womb when she is surrounded by an army of upwardly mobile black economic empowerment moguls in a boardroom, focusing exclusively on the market?

As women move into historically masculine territories, we have to do so in ways that do not oppress our female nature. By saying that, I am neither advocating that women be sent back home to breed children, nor claiming that menstruation is a time for women to be treated with kid gloves. As we stand up against the image of womanhood painted by patriarchy, we have to be vigilant so as to avoid falling into the trap of feminine suppression. The question is: can we be feminist and feminine?

In her book *Honoring Menstruation*[2], Lara Owen asserts that PMS should stand for pre-menstrual strength, because in a society that thrives on appointments, deadlines and schedules, it forces women to shift their attention to their bodies. Such a shift, she argues, forces the woman to be conscious of her emotions and her power in a society that expects women to hold in so much for peace's sake. A roadmap to peace in this instance is derived from an underlying fear of being labelled a bad mother, an uncaring wife, an irrational boss or a matriarch whose mission in life is to castrate as many men as possible. Instead of experiencing PMS as a nuisance, Owen argues that women should see it as

[2] Owen, L. 1998. *Honoring Menstruation: A Time of Self-Renewal.* Freedom, Calif.: The Crossing Press.

potentially useful. After all, she says, it opens our emotions and makes it hard for us to suppress our feelings, needs and discomforts. In her book *Women's Bodies, Women's Wisdom*[3], Dr Christiane Northrup concurs, viewing menstruation as being as natural to a woman's body as the ebb and flow of ocean tides are to nature. The ripening and release of the egg, the change of seasons as well as the waxing and waning of the moon all represent a cyclical connection to Mother Earth.

In a world where multitudes of women are more closely connected to pharmaceutical companies (which supply them with contraceptives, painkillers, tranquillisers and hormone replacements) than to nature, Northrup urges women to rethink menstruation as a powerful and deeply suppressed part of the feminine archetype. Once we embrace menstruation as part of our femaleness, our healing will begin.

The process of healing my menstrual rage started in earnest in 2000 after I resigned as director of ADAPT, a women's organisation that I had founded and directed for nine years. After years of running, fighting, lobbying and accumulating a sizeable amount of personal and national rage, the time had come for me to let go of almost everything that I owned, including my house, my vehicle (which I lost in a horrific accident) and my title of Director. The only title I could not peel off was that of mother. I set out to settle in a place surrounded by mountains, lakes and rivers, miles away from the soul-wrenching pace of life in the big city. In addition to satisfying a deep longing to return to Mother Earth for spiritual recovery and discovery, my choice of a place far removed from the people I had worked with for so many years was meant to help me learn to say no. It was so

[3] Northrup, C. 2000. *Women's Bodies, Women's Wisdom*. Revised edition. London: Piatkus.

much easier to turn down a request with "I don't live in Jo'burg any more".

The first few months of rest were painful. For the first time in a long time I kept my own company, consciously reflecting on my life as a woman, mother, lover, activist, healer, writer, poet and dancer (this last persona having remained suppressed, waiting in the wings). My efforts at putting the pieces of my life together were greatly enhanced by literature on women and spirituality, as well as earth-based wisdom that I accumulated from rural women, with whom I was in constant contact. My reading introduced me to the idea of keeping a moon journal, which helped me to record the effects of my menstrual cycle on my life.

By keeping track of the phases of the moon, I reclaimed my cyclical connection with the moon and nature. One evening, while doing a full moon meditation, with India Arie singing "Beautiful" and my blood flowing freely, I cried a river of tears held back for a long time. I cried in pain as I released the conditioning I had accepted, that had made me a strong woman expected to "act like a man". I cried because the answers to questions I asked about my life presented themselves with shocking clarity. I cried in deep appreciation of the overwhelming love of Moon the Goddess.

My reconnection with nature and my menstrual cycle has turned my menstrual rage to menstrual creative power. I find inspiration to write some of my best poetry and essays when I am menstruating at full moon. My moon time at full moon is a time of heightened creativity. By honouring my blood, I welcome the reminder that birth always follows death. Now that I am familiar with my moods and behavioural patterns just before the onset of my menstruation, instead of fighting the energy, I work with it. Even though I grew up thinking that I should have been a boy, as an adult, I simply adore the fact that I am woman. How could I have even thought of asking for anything less than to be a custodian of feminine power?

Feminine power, however, is not restricted to menstruation and childbirth. During a seminar entitled "Rethinking menstruation as a female experience", which I conducted at Wits University in the second half of 2002, I was asked what happens to the menopausal woman. Does the fact that she has stopped menstruating mean that she no longer has creative power?

In our patriarchal and ageist culture, menopause is viewed with a negativity based largely on society's conception of a woman as a bearer of children. Since the menopausal woman can no longer give birth, she is cast aside. Since society tends to measure beauty in terms of a woman's ability to attract a man, a woman with withered breasts and a flabby pouch for a tummy is no longer viewed as attractive. Manipulating such stereotypes and women's fear of ageing, pharmaceutical companies set out to design messages that reinforce the belief that the menopausal woman's body and mind will fall apart unless she takes medication. Yet menopause, just like puberty and pregnancy, is a natural phase that involves change. Just like any other phase, menopause is a time to reconnect with yet another layer of a woman's power. On being asked what it felt like to be 70, Maya Angelou replied "70 is hot". Even though her breasts were racing to see which one would reach her waist first, she felt whole, beautiful, and full of creative energy. Indeed, beauty is in the eye of the internal beholder, and is not confined to the exterior. My image of a sexy woman embraces Toni Morrison's grey locks and her eloquence, as well as Nomzamo Madikizela-Mandela's presence and grace. The beauty of older women resides not just in the physical, but also in their mental and spiritual freedom.

Living life to the fullest

Something I love about my life is the fact that I can get up in Johannesburg in the morning, enjoy a breakfast of fruit and juice, then get into my car and in a relatively short time find myself in a rural village sitting on a bench under a tree eating porridge and sour milk with an elder, such as my grandfather.

Unlike a Western meal, where you don't leave the table until you have finished eating, meals with my grandfather are typically interrupted by having to chase the goats, which find his crops irresistible. The goats having been chased off with the help of a long home-made whip, a further interruption to our lunch may present itself in the form of two old women, who stop to greet us and inquire about our well-being. After responding to their enquiry and asking about their health, grandfather introduces me as Rantebo's first child, announcing proudly that I have driven a car alone all the way from Johannesburg to spend the day with him. They in turn, tell about someone who was killed in a nearby village, narrating the cause of his death in detail. Listening to their conversation, I wonder how on earth they could have gathered so much information about the event. Talk about investigative journalism! Having passed on the news, they wish us good health and leave. Only then do we return to what is left of our lunch.

Now, if you were to participate in such an action-packed lunch, what would your approach to table manners be? Would you honestly be concerned about the difference between a dessert spoon and a tablespoon? Would you really care whether a particular knife is supposed to be used for steak or fish? The fact that there are different types of glasses for red and white wine would be completely irrelevant if you were drinking *mageu* in a calabash. It's all a question of the finer things in life.

When we talk of the finer things in life, don't we usually mean the finer things in Western life? So often, when we reflect on our modern lives, we are quick to say we have come too far to go back. Does that make us powerless in the mighty grip of consumerism? Or is it possible to enjoy all that a modern lifestyle has to offer without losing our essence? What is our essence?

As a way of exploring these issues, I'd like to return to a day spent with my beloved grandfather. I left Johannesburg after ten in the morning to visit him in Bollantlokwe. Just before reaching Tladistad, I drove past my dad in his battered Toyota Stallion, accompanied by some old men from Kgomo Kgomo. I stopped briefly to greet them and learnt that they had just come back from "a meeting of the cows" in a nearby village. After a brief stop at Dikebu to see my aunt, I finally arrived in Bollantlokwe just after two in the afternoon. Following custom, I announced my presence by calling "*Ka mo gae*" whilst still some distance from the door, and heard him respond in the house. I found him stretched comfortably on an old sofa, which obviously has many stories to tell, like so much of the old furniture that some white people continue to take from our elders for nothing, only to refurbish and sell for thousands in their trendy antique shops and tea gardens. I have, on occasion, seen dealers driving out of remote villages with trailers full of these priceless pieces of furniture. In most instances, cheap plastic replacements will take their place.

While these valuable assets are taken from our villages, we in turn load our vans with discarded empty drums, plastic containers, broken bicycles, old broken beds and "kitchen schemes" from white people's homes and bring them to our villages around the Easter and Christmas holidays. This practice of giving up our assets for unwanted rubbish makes my heart bleed. And the practice of taking people's most valuable possessions takes many forms.

My grandfather Ramokotong is the brother of my paternal grandfather, Ramoloi Mosire Motsei. He lived through the infamous World War II, and explains that when they came to recruit men to fight in the war, he was not in the village at the time. Had it not been for that, he would be dead, like his contemporaries who fought in the war.

Although a little frail, he is well. On the day of my visit he recognised me without needing spectacles, and beamed, revealing one prominent tooth that refuses to let go. In spite of his age my grandfather remains active, engaging and energetic. Watching him on that day made me deeply proud to be a woman in modern Africa. Due to his age, he is slightly hunched, and I found myself imagining how good looking he must have been when he was young. Men from the Motsei clan are known to be tall, good-looking and gentle. I am a bit reluctant to use the term "gentlemen" to describe them, though, because

I am not really sure of what the English had in mind when they coined the term.

Coming as I do from a family of good-looking, tall black men, can anyone blame me for having ventured into the world searching for nothing less than a tall and beautiful black man to sweep me off my feet? Can anyone blame me for my repeated hit-and-miss escapades that had very little to do with an appreciation of inner beauty? When you are young and in search of a companion, the external tends to take precedence. It is only later in life that you come to notice and enjoy the other's inner being. But by the time you realise that the inner being is more of a jewel than meets the eye, you will have made a fair number of mistakes. I have become wiser by learning from my mistakes. The ability to enjoy the other, inner beauty comes from discovering your own. I love who I have become. No, I love who I am becoming. Life is an evolving journey; we are forever becoming.

In 1924 my grandfather married Mokotji Phallane, who was born in the village of Modubung in the district of Belabela, previously known as Warmbaths, and they were blessed with eight children. The name "Belabela" comes from the Setswana verb *"go bela"*, which means "to boil", and refers to the natural warm springs in the area, a natural resource that Mother Nature has given abundantly to be enjoyed by all. Yet some individuals saw fit to design a resort and make a living out of what was meant for all of us. Many of the children living in the vicinity of the mineral baths have never set foot in the resort. A lucky few get to visit it once a year, on New Year's Day. Sadly, this natural resource has now become a facility enjoyed exclusively by those who can afford to pay for timeshare and other exclusive holiday packages. Tourism and an appreciation for the environment have become a pastime for the elite minority.

My grandfather spent the greater part of his working life as a chef for one Mr George Shaw, who lived on the corner of Goldreich and Claim Streets in Hillbrow. George Shaw was an English barrister who was responsible for the allocation of houses in Sophiatown. My grandfather speaks fondly of Mr Shaw, and tells that at one time he wanted to build him a house in Sophiatown. However, my grandfather's father, who was in Bollantlokwe, would not hear of his grandchildren growing up without a rural base.

On the day of my visit, I asked my grandfather how he accounted for having lived so long. Two factors, he replied: healthy eating habits, which are common in traditional African societies, and the golden rule – respect for the elders.

He also told me about his role as *Kgosana* responsible for the administration of village affairs in the district of Mosetlha, the original name for Makapanstad. With a deep sense of pride, he recalled how dedicated his contemporaries were to the advancement and quality of life in the villages. From my early years I clearly remember the motto *"Re tla direla"*, which was meant to instil a spirit of self-reliance and good governance amongst my people.

These days we hear endless accusations of ineffective and undemocratic governance in Africa, yet no-one takes into consideration the negative impact of the colonial attitudes and practices of Western countries whose governments are being paraded as models of excellence. Every time I see television images of loud-mouthed, finger-wagging First World leaders publicly lying about global attacks on civilisation and freedom, I can't think of anything else to do but laugh in their faces. Their time will come. The truth always triumphs.

As he told the story, my grandfather got up to show me two photographs of *Kgosi* Seaparankwe Makapan and *Kgosi* Nchaupe Makapan. He once had a visit from men closely related to the royal kraal, who wanted to take the photographs. They couldn't understand why he should keep such treasures when he had no close association to royalty. He soon put them right, explaining that he was not just a dedicated citizen of the village, but that his mother, Mamoleke Makapan, was from the royal family.

I also learnt from him that my great-great-grandfather, Poo Ramokolokolo Manyane, who left Lehurutshe to avoid a war, was of royal origin. He came to Mosetlha and was given the role of making fire at the chief's kraal, *motsei wa mollo*.

Mogolo kenosi wa ba Manyane maya bokgolwa go ya go tlhama lesika la ba RaMotsei a Manyane. Ke kgakgathiba ya bo Serake serakalela letsibogong la boNkoto. Ke setlola mafura a phofu, mafura a kgama, mafura a sebata segolo ntswe a tshwene a le teng. Setlola mafura a motlhouwane a ntseng le a tlola mekokotlo dipale badidi e tswe a tlola ke Poo Ramokololo. Kgomo lla!!!

My paternal grandmother Mmatshilo's mother, Mankoko, was a princess of the Matlala monarchy known to live adjacent to an ancestral mountain called Thaba Mogosi.

Motho was bo Tlhankga a mehlaba, o ana nonyana,
ke tlhantlhagane e kgolo, ke tlhantlhagane ya Mogosi,
Ke thaba ya Badimo le batho. Mogosi a Mmatlala.
Batho ba rile ba re fora ba re thaba yeso ga e
namelwe, ra e namela ra e fologa, ra e fologa ka
morago.

Great-great-grandmother Mma Matlala is my link
with my Pedi ancestry. She married a Mokgatla man,
Ramogomotsi Moloisane, who was said to be so huge
that he could single-handedly pull a bull down to its
slaughter, holding on to its horns. Their daughter was
Mmatshilo Moloisane, my father's mother.

Motho wa boMpadia thata a maiyane, o iphara sesadi
marumong, o iphara sesetsanyana motsopye,
mosetsana wa mereleba, a re le se nnyatseng mmala
mofitshwana, rona batsopye ga re ikgalale, ga re
ikgalale e bile ga re ipelaele.

I left grandfather late in the afternoon, stopping to
pick up a stone at his gate to put on my ancestral shrine
at my home in Johannesburg. Instead of heading straight
back home, I decided to drive through Kgomo Kgomo to
spend some time with my parents. I reflected on the
stories that grandfather had shared with me, and on what
he had had to say about traditional, healthy eating habits.
Soul food from the soil.

They did not just take our land from us. They also
took our indigenous ways of farming, only to repackage
them and give them foreign labels such as
"permaculture", "organic farming" and "sustainable
agriculture". Surely, if we were dependent upon Nature

in the way that our foremothers and forefathers were, there would not be a way of tilling our lands without giving back to the Source. Yes, our ancestors were unlettered in the Western sense, but their spiritual connection to the earth and all that lives on it served as a mighty Open University.

As I reflected about food and nutrition, I thought of the fine job corporations and junk food outlets are doing in creating a global culture of malnutrition. While these international giants have a reputation for marketing excellence and sizeable social responsibility programmes, what is not mentioned is their long-term impact on the quality of the life of the majority of the poor. I have interacted with women participating in microfinance schemes intended to alleviate widespread poverty in the rural areas, and it has been impossible not to notice the deliberate dislocation between the lending process and broader development imperatives. The commodities that these women eventually sell, alcohol and fizzy drinks, create addiction and dependency, and have no human or social value.

We are faced with the challenge of opening avenues that encourage indigenous communities to rediscover culturally embedded methods of production and consumption. Rising to this challenge implies acknowledging the failure of development imperatives based exclusively on models derived from Western market economies, whose primary goals are profit maximisation and capital accumulation.

Economic instability in Africa is only ever attributed to corrupt governance. While some governments in Africa are corrupt, certainly, current analysis of the economic situation in the region chooses to overlook corporations that continue to drain and channel dividends from local subsidiaries to international conglomerates. We are a nation that does not believe in itself, a continent that still looks up to the West, particularly the European Union and United States, as our economic and spiritual saviours. It is no wonder that we are so drained, so lost.

I arrived at my parents' home and joined in their conversation under a *Motlopi* tree. I shared the stories told by grandfather, and what he had had to say about the notion of the earth revolving around the sun. "White people seem to think that we have no brains", he had said. "We first moved from Suiwerskuil in 1915 and I have been living in the same house for years. I never woke up in the morning to find this house in Moretele (a nearby village). Even this house next door, it has always been in this position. Not once did I get up in the morning to find it in front of our gate. Now, you tell me, is it the sun or the earth that is moving?"

I left to the sound of my father's fond laughter in response to the logic behind this philosophical, if not geographical, wisdom, and drove back to Johannesburg from Kgomo Kgomo listening to Segale Mogotsi of Kaya FM playing the discs of yesterday. Pretending to be Brenda Fassie (who cares, there's no-one listening!), I sang along at the top of my voice, tapping my fingers on the steering wheel in a way that would rival that fine drummer Mabe Thobejane.

At home, I recounted grandfather's stories of our foremothers and forefathers to my children, and experienced the light in their eyes and their appreciative laughter as testimony to the healing power of storytelling.

May stories of love and care, peace and health, abundance and spiritual wealth, good governance and self-reliance in Africa continue to be told across generations and centuries.

NKOSI SIKELELA.

Parents and parenting

This chapter is meant as a sharing of my philosophy of parenting. My focus, though, will be on mothers raising children on their own. This is a deliberate choice, based on my personal experience. However, while I feel that the majority of men do not play a significant role in parenting, I by no means mean to dismiss the handful of men who choose to raise children on their own. As a society, we know very little about the challenges that these men face as single parents, and I hope that as more is written about their experiences we will be able to correct the common myth that parenting is an exclusively female responsibility. The choices and experiences of some caring fathers are living proof that men can and should participate actively in raising children.

What does single parenting mean in an African context? Single parenthood in our communities goes beyond the situation where a man has died, divorced or even deserted his wife and family. In a country whose riches have been built on a foundation of influx control and a migrant labour system, many women in rural South Africa have to contend with raising children on their own. For many black children, their relationship with their father is limited to irregular visits from a man who is almost a stranger to them.

This is a phenomenon that is not exclusive to working-class fathers. Increasing numbers of middle-class fathers are leaving home in pursuit of wealth and/or fame, to spend their time and energy chasing empowerment deals and deadlines. In the process, many succumb to poor health worsened by stress, chronic fatigue, weight problems and dependence on substances such as alcohol. While it is true that in the past many black fathers died of tuberculosis compounded by malnutrition and other preventable poverty-related diseases, lately diseases of privilege seem to be becoming increasingly prevalent.

Despite achieving apparent success and wealth, people aren't happy. Suicide and heart attacks have become the order of the day. Political and business leadership is in disarray. There are enough indications at both micro and macro level that we need to engage in a reflective process that will integrate success with harmony and balance in the home and in society, and provide a sense of spiritual fulfilment and inner peace. Men know that sooner or later they will be forced to consider such a path; the future of our boys depends on it.

Single parenting may also result from ill health and disability in a country whose health and social services are skewed towards those who can afford to pay. Fathers may look physically fit, but display symptoms of spiritual ill health resulting from a past characterised by deprivation, discrimination and the erosion of personal integrity and dignity. This is reflected in the increasing rate of divorce, addiction to alcohol, drugs, work and gambling, as well as societal violence, which has resulted in a great many black men languishing in the country's overcrowded prisons. All of these and many other related factors have landed us in a situation where the majority of children grow up without a father's love, guidance and counsel.

Overall, the state of fatherhood needs urgent attention. This won't be easy, though, given that our society seems to encourage the situation I have just described. We live in a country that believes in building more casinos and prisons than schools and arts centres. As a country, we believe in the lie that a casino will contribute positively to the economy of the country, and we fail to acknowledge the detrimental long-term effects on the psyche of the people. Surely healthy economic growth must bring with it long-term observable improvements in the level of happiness and well-being (including a positive self-identity) for the majority of people? As a nation, we cannot just be content with unprecedented economic growth without examining whether that growth is pathological or disruptive.

While political and economic factors contribute to the way families operate these days, it isn't enough that a father's contribution to the lives of his children should be limited to money. What is needed is an emotional connection with the children, and a better quantity and quality of time devoted to domestic responsibilities. Fathering seems to be equated with no more than an occasional visit to a movie rather than with fundamental, day-to-day physical and psychological parenting responsibilities. In the literal and figurative absence of fathers, single mothers have done a great job in many instances. But at what cost?

Am I a single mother? I have often asked myself this question, and in the end have come up with a many-facetted answer. Yes, I am a single mother by virtue of having been divorced and having my children live with me, without the constant physical presence of a father. However, I do not feel that I am raising the children on my own. Firstly, I am blessed in that the children's fathers take an active role in connecting and bonding with their children, and so the children's interaction with their fathers is not limited to a bank transfer at the end of each month or an occasional drive to Milky Lane for an ice-cream. But this situation was not presented to me on a platter just like that. I have earned it. I had to learn to communicate.

Communication is a great deal more than just talking; it involves listening to and understanding the other person's point of view, and saying what you really mean. Communicating truthfully and honestly also means accepting that your view may not necessarily be the right one. Learning all that took a great deal of effort, energy and time. For me, it was a difficult but worthwhile journey.

As a mother, I have to confess that there have been times when I used the children to fight my battles. There have also been times when I have taken out my anger and frustrations on them. While I did not hit them physically, there are things that I said or did that hurt them. And that means that I in fact abused them emotionally. "Abuse" is a very strong word to use in this instance, especially coming from me, a woman who has dedicated the greater part of her life fighting all forms of violence in the home. However, I use the word deliberately as a way of taking full responsibility for the hurt that I caused my children. I was in pain, certainly, but that was no excuse for hurting those that I love most.

Admitting to one's dark side and bringing it out into the open is not a pleasant thing to do. It requires telling the truth, and that makes it uncomfortable. But why should telling the truth be uncomfortable? Why should we be comfortable with not telling the truth? Is not telling the truth the same thing as lying? What is truth?

This last question sent me to the writings of some of the spiritual guides that I have relied on over time. After some inconclusive searching I turned to Gary Zukav's *The Seat of the Soul*, in which he specifically enquires about the nature of truth. Zukav answers his question (and mine) by describing truth as "that which does not contaminate you, but empowers you. Therefore, there are degrees of truth, but, generically, truth is that which can do no harm. It cannot harm".[4]

I then turned to *The Art of Harmony* by Sang H. Kim[5], and found an answer early in the first chapter – he describes truth as reunion with the original self, and asserts that because truth is at our core, it is often hidden by many layers and that we need patience, will and wisdom to uncover it. One who has attained truth is a person of freedom.

If truth is a reunion with who we are, why does it take us so long to find it? If truth is the path to freedom, what makes it difficult for us to embrace it fully? After all, we all want to be free. In fact, truth is inherent in all of us, and we all know what it is. We all have a conscience playing the role of a guardian angel steering us toward our truth. Are we open enough, silent enough and conscious enough to feel, hear and see the manifestations of the truth in our lives? In essence, I did not really have to scout for my answer in written texts; I had it inside me the whole time. We all do.

But getting back to whether I am a single mother or not; yes, on the one hand, and no on the other, because the family that consists of myself and my children rests on a very strong foundation of extended family support.

[4] Zukav, G. 1998. *The Seat of the Soul*. London: Rider Books: pp.69–70.
[5] Kim, S.H. 2001. *The Art of Harmony*. 2nd edition. Hartford CT: Turtle Press: p.29.

My parents are active grandparents, my brothers Mosire, Manyane and Serake take their role as uncles very seriously, and my sister Lenyalo and I raise our children together. At school, when asked whether he has siblings, my sister's only child, Kgosietsile, says that he has, as he views my children as his brothers and sister.

I am grateful for such love and support. There have been so many parenting challenges that I could not have dealt with on my own. Parenting is a full-time, high-stress job, which is almost impossible for one person alone – there are instances where even two parents don't know what to do or say. In the past, this is where the extended family would intervene. It has been at times when the men in my life – my father, brothers (including my brother-in-law) and partner – stepped in to defuse an incendiary situation between this single mother and her eldest son that I have realised the shortcomings of a family consisting of children and just one parent.

Whatever happened to our indigenous ways of raising children? What happened to the wisdom accumulated by our foreparents over centuries? Why are we so taken with Piaget's theory of child development that we fail to evaluate it within our own cultural context? I have to admit, however, that an exercise of this kind would prove difficult, if not impossible, with so many of our children barely speaking their native languages.

Black parents with children in the so-called white schools will have experienced the dilemma of dealing with a child who not only spends time in a different world, but also uses a different language to express himself or herself. Cultural values are conveyed through language. Language is a powerful tool of self-definition.

By conceptualising in a foreign language at school, our children participate in a different world of experiences from that of their immediate family and community. The fact that our children have been prised loose from our immediate environment poses fundamental parenting challenges.

As modern black parents who have been raised differently, how do we guide without being prescriptive? How do we reconcile the modern concept of freedom of speech and a culture of rights with the traditional notion of respect for elders? How can we learn and teach the art of saying no without being disrespectful to our elders? How do we integrate the wisdom embedded in sayings such as *"Lore lo ojwa le sa le metsi"* and *"Mafura a ngwana ke go rongwa"* into modern parenting principles? Is it possible to help our children to embrace their identity through music, dance and oral history using a foreign language?

Many of us have commented on how our children tend to communicate in English even while playing amongst themselves at extended family gatherings. We feel keenly about this, yet we laugh and find solace in the saying *"Leso legolo ditshego"*. While this may work in the short term, leaving these seeds to grow may well result in a bitter harvest.

While operating with the support of an extended family is ideal, it becomes most effective if all parties work together in a way that reflects mutual respect. To achieve that, we all need to learn to influence and be influenced, and to be willing to make compromises as well as have the courage to acknowledge that we have made mistakes. This is essential if we are to provide positive role models for our children.

Providing positive role models for our children will not be easy given the high prevalence of divorce. These days, a significant number of children are raised in more than one household by different sets of guardians. We would like to believe that our children are coping – and that includes having to forgive us for our imperfections, particularly when it comes to our intimate relationships. More often than not, they meet and get emotionally attached to several strangers in their mother's life. Boys may respond by becoming overprotective, and developing an aversion to their mother's partner. Single mothers need to stop and critically examine the challenges in our lives. We need to reflect on ways of making the best of our lives as single women and as mothers in this most challenging era of societal transition.

Black single mothers may find that even though they may have given it their all against all odds, their children are nevertheless deeply wounded. Our juvenile prisons are full of black boys being moulded into men. Instead of being embraced in the love, guidance and care of their guardians, they are sodomised and brutalised. A significant number have never laid their eyes on the man whose blood run through their veins. While they try hard to be "real men" and pretend to be tough, as they lie awake at night in an overcrowded cell with bodies that are as ravaged as their souls, many long for the father they never had.

Those of us who are single mothers are faced with a massive responsibility amidst uncertainty, pain, desperation and the sense of bearing a heavy burden. Many of us have drawn strength from the saying *"Kgomo ga e ke e imelwa ke morwalo e le wa yona"*. More often than not, we long for love, happiness and support without realising that true love and happiness grow from self-love and inner peace. By advocating self-love, I am not in any way suggesting arrogance or a lack of compassion. Healthy self-love comes from our ability to face our imperfections and heal our wounded psyche. Such a process involves a humble and yet realistic estimation of our true worth and abilities. Where there is a need for us to change, let us have the courage to do so. If this includes facing our tendency to take out anger for their fathers' absence on our boys, we should face that reality without shame. It is with this release that we can learn the art of asking for help whenever we need it instead of being buried in a heap of self-pity or arrogant but empty pride.

I have a teenage son to raise and learn from. Katlego is not a typical macho teenager, and he has challenged my concept of parenting in many ways. He has never lived physically with his biological father, and is struggling to find himself. I also have a younger son, and in the four short years of his life, Onkgopotse has already claimed his rightful place as my teacher.

I am grateful for the opportunity to learn the art of parenting. Drawing on my knowledge of project management, I am only too aware that as a parent one does not have the option of "going back to the drawing board" if a project does not go according to plan. Parenting is a project that involves striving to do your very best all the time because if your son turns 16 and is filled with so much self-hatred that he lands up in trouble, it isn't always possible to go back and start over. I don't mean that there isn't room for mistakes. However, parenting calls for living life in the present.

Yesterday belongs in our past and there is nothing that we can do to change it. Instead of spending time worrying about a past that we can never alter, we are better off focusing on a future that we have the power to influence. This future, however, does not begin tomorrow, or even in five minutes' time, but right now.

I have been significantly influenced by a Buddhist way of living documented in contemporary writings of authors such as Jon Kabat-Zinn, who views parenting as a mindful and spiritual practice. In his book *Wherever You Go, There You Are* [6], Kabat-Zinn views children as our own private mindfulness teachers who have been brought into our lives for a purpose and whose presence and actions are guaranteed to push all our sensitive and hidden buttons. This, he asserts, give us a never-ending range of opportunities to recognise our limitations and attachments. He sees parenting as a high-pressure job that calls for us to be observant and learn from our children – a task that gets more challenging as the children grow and develop their own ideas and viewpoints.

Being able to live physically with our children and therefore learn by observation is complicated by the fact that many parents have biological children from more than one relationship. The general trend is to dismiss parents with children from more than one relationship as having no morals. However, the current state of well-being in our families does not grant any of us licence to take the moral high ground without acknowledging the reality of high divorce rates and other factors. The current state of the family, whatever its configuration and composition, calls for a collective, intense and in-depth exploration of the possible answers to the complex questions facing us today.

Some of the answers may lie in eliminating any economic and social structure that keeps men from being

[6] Kabat-Zinn, J. 1995. *Wherever You Go, There You Are: Mindfulness Meditation in Everyday Life*. USA: Hyperion.

actively involved in the lives of their children. Modern society often tends to reward men for overwork, feeding them the message that tangible economic outputs are more valuable than their presence at home as nurturing fathers. Other answers may be found in applying some of our ancient socio-cultural wisdom in order to solve modern problems. A renewal of our subscription to the age-old belief that it takes a village to raise a child may assist in reclaiming the collective responsibility that each adult has towards their biological and non-biological children. Yet other answers lie in the individual. For instance, many adults of my generation have children from more than one partner without having married them. Already, a significant number of young people are following in our footsteps. Unfortunately, it is often the children who ultimately suffer. They are expected to make a life founded on their parents' past errors of judgement.

Increasing access to birth control has brought with it an increasing inability to control birth. Besides, the phenomenon of childbirth is as much a man's responsibility as it is a woman's. I often encourage my son never to put his life in the hands of another individual. I emphasise that a decision whether or not to have a child out of wedlock lies squarely with him; he alone is responsible for pursuing his dreams and goals. Discussions about teenage pregnancy hardly ever include teenage fathers, which means that young men are excluded from a fundamental life education process that has a crucial bearing on their future.

As a nation, we endeavour to fight corruption and greed in our political and economic institutions, yet we fail to accept that our attitude to sex comes from the same source, a dis-eased soul. We rationalise promiscuity as a demonstration of an evolved and liberated personality. A continued refusal to do inner consciousness work is reflected in our tendency to hold up the condom, often imported from foreign governments at a cost of billions of rands, as an answer to HIV/Aids prevention. All that that little piece of rubber does is inhibit physical contact – it has no power to change a course of action. For that you need the power of the mind and heart. Advocates of the exclusive use of condoms are not interested in finding a lasting solution that comes from the full realisation that outcomes in our lives are the result of our choices. Much as we are products of our past, we all have the intelligence and the capacity to make life-affirming choices that influence our future positively.

I applaud the work that single mothers have done in raising their children through years of immense sacrifice. While acknowledging that these mothers have made the best of their circumstances amidst financial and other constraints, we cannot leave the entire responsibility of raising children to them alone. A father's contribution and influence is essential. I urge fathers (biological and non-biological) to take their rightful place in taking care of their children. I also urge mothers to heal their wounds and redefine what being a good mother is all about. Being ruled by pride and not asking for help and support does not make us good mothers. Women and men need to work together for the survival of the species and the planet. In my view, there will never be a more effective crime prevention strategy than effective parenting.

It is time to bring the age of absent fathers to an end. We are no longer interested in media reports about fathers, even those tasked with the responsibility of leading the country, failing in their role as leaders in their own homes. The current attitude towards and practice of child support does little to reconstruct and reweave the ravaged threads of our families and communities. Child support should be a demonstration of compassion and the acceptance of responsibility for a soul that came through our bodies. It is a serious indictment on us that we have to rely on an Act of Parliament and the courts to enforce loving and caring for our children. The amount of money, time and energy that we spend on tracing absent fathers and engaging with the legal system to enforce something that should come naturally is utterly wasteful. We could be spending such resources on many other developmental priorities that our country is faced with.

We are faced with the challenge of transforming the family into a unit that provides full support for our children. I call on parents to make a commitment and take a stand in support of family and community reconstruction. Taking a stand begins with our own healing. We cannot allow past errors to ruin events in our future. It is always possible to make a new beginning.

A black man with soul

It is April 2000. I am in New York, and I have just met a delightful black man. I found it refreshing to meet a man of African descent who knows and is passionate about who he really is in spite of a simple and poor childhood. He feels and looks solid, sturdy, dependable and self-assured. He is passionate about being an African. A visiting professor of African history at one of the leading institutions in the West, his passion for Africa emanates not only from his ancestry but also from the time he spent teaching in Nigeria, Tanzania and Zimbabwe.

It was his silence that first struck me. He communicates through his silence; he is a great listener too. It was only after I got off at my station and was walking to my hotel room in the early hours of the morning that I began to ponder on the power that comes with being a good listener. On our subway journey back from the Museum of African Art, he let me talk endlessly about my work and myself until we got to my stop. I could not believe that I had been so self-centred, raving only about the things that I do, things that light my fire. When we parted, we agreed that we would meet again before I headed out to Washington DC. I made a pact with myself: the next time I met him, I would listen more.

Our evening had been delightful, spiced with music served by a band from Cameroon. The lead guitarist was also a professor of African history. I so enjoyed their discussion about the fusion of African history and music. It was a beautiful encounter with two sons of the soil, one raised in Trinidad and the other in Cameroon.

The next evening we met for dinner and he treated me to Caribbean delicacies, which we enjoyed against a backdrop of live music. I learnt that he was married with two children – he described himself as a man for whom family means everything. He was on sabbatical, had been away from his family for some time, and was looking forward to going back home in a few weeks. A black man devoted to his family – yet another cause for celebration.

We are constantly bombarded with images of irresponsible black men who are full of a self-hatred that makes them incapable of taking care of themselves and their families. Whether true or contrived, these images have to be tackled constructively if we are to re-cast fathers in their central role in child development. It was as a result of this encounter, and of course my personal experience of a father who has always been there for me, that I returned to my idea of initiating a "best fathers" project in Alexandra Township. A caring black father from the ghetto – a truly healing and liberating image.

Our discussion that evening was as delightful and intense as the food and the music. We explored the difficulties faced by African parents who want to raise their children unpoisoned by Western ideology in an era perceived as technologically advanced. We both felt strongly about the role of language in shaping our children's identity. I shared with him that even though my children attend a so-called white school, they know and understand the role of Setswana in their lives. Further into our discussion, we spoke of the role of music in the liberation of Africans. I was fascinated by the fact that he plays Bob Marley in his history class to make a point about African revolution. We spoke about Marcus Garvey, Aime Cesaire, Malcolm X, Steve Biko, Fela Kuti. I commented on the silence about and lack of documentation on the contribution of women in African history and he agreed.

Why would I want to know about Joan of Arc when I could be learning about Yaa Asantewaa, an Ashanti woman who led her people into battle during the Anglo-Ashanti war in Ghana in 1900? Closer to home, there is a record of women warriors in the old kingdom of Monomotapa, and of the shaman warrior woman, Mbuya Nehanda, who led the Shona in a war of liberation in the late 19th century. Why is it then that the role of African women in African civilisation and liberation has been almost obliterated? Surely there is no reason for me to be fascinated by the powers of the Greek goddesses when the concept of Goddess the creator, mother of all people, is common throughout Africa? Other than Goddess the creator, there are goddesses for every aspect of life and living in African mythology. There is Moon the Goddess, goddesses of divine wisdom, childbirth, rain, healing, and moral judgement, as well as river goddesses revered for their generosity. In Africa we need to remember the powerful role of women as queens, both as rulers in their own right as well as holders of the position of queen mother, with the power to select a new king. In spite of a reported preference for boy children in some African cultures, others place a high value on girl babies. We have internalised so many of the lies and distortions.

There is no doubt that the revival of an African Renaissance supported by current initiatives such as NEPAD and the African Union should return women to their rightful place. It is clear from history that the role of women as political decision-makers and traders in pre-colonial Africa has been adversely affected by colonial occupation. Drawing women from the fringes and back into the centre of African civilisation will go a long way towards restoring the facts distorted first by those who came to colonise and later by African historians who seem happy to rewrite history as if there have never been any women in Africa.

The evening ended with a visit to a bookshop, where he bought me a copy of Miles Davis's autobiography and inscribed it, "For a spirit child, filled with all that African jazz". I know that I may never meet this man again. I also know that I will never forget our conversation. I returned to my hotel room glowing like the woman in Maya Angelou's poem "Phenomenal woman". I went to bed thinking of yet another black man, my beloved mentor and Africanist father, Esk'ia Mphahlele. Africa my music.

Postscript: I had just finished reworking my original journal entry to create this chapter when my son, Onkgopotse, woke up for one of his midnight cuddles. His timing could not have been better. I took him in my arms and kissed his forehead. I stroked his African hair and the texture felt so tight, so real. I have a theory that you can always tell if someone was kissed a lot when she or he was a baby. I am raising a black man and I cannot help wondering how he will turn out later in his life. As a black woman who is committed to the survival of the species, I will give him as much love as I possess. While I know that ultimately his future is in his hands, I am so very aware of my role in building the foundation that will be the base from which he will operate. I promise to do the best I can.

Together, Onkgopotse and I danced to the land of our ancestors, *re isa marapo go beng,* to the accompaniment of Paul Hanmer's "Trains to Taung". His electric conversations with Louis Mhlanga go right to the core of my being. Africa is my rhythm, Africa is my blues.

My work, my life

When I resigned from my position as research officer at the University of the Witwatersrand at the end of 1990, although driven by my personal experience of abuse and my past experience as a nurse working in an emergency ward treating countless women who had survived horrendous injuries at the hands of men who professed to love them, I had no more than a vague idea of the path that lay ahead of me. As I began my work in the field of domestic violence in Africa, based in Alexandra Township, my greatest challenge lay in finding solutions that were not just culturally acceptable and relevant, but effective in reducing the epidemic. It was imperative to take a stand against violence in the home, yet avoid contributing to the annihilation of the black family.

As a researcher and citizen of the world I have encountered horrific accounts of the sexual torture of women and children in the name of global economic growth. I have been involved in advocating a change in perceptions and attitudes toward women on a continent ravaged by poverty and war, with women raped and molested in great numbers. The experience I have gained has been a vital source of personal growth.

I am always asked: Why Alexandra? I was first introduced to Alexandra Township when I was working as a junior research officer at the Centre for Health Policy of the Department of Community Health at Wits

Medical School. One of my duties included accompanying fourth-year medical students on field trips to Alexandra Health and University Clinic as well as through the township itself. It was during this time that I was exposed to the gross deprivation that the majority of people experienced and the squalor in which they were (and still are) expected to live.

With my rural upbringing, I had never before been exposed to urban degradation. While I was deeply affected by the appalling living conditions to which a great number of South Africans were subjected, I was at the same time moved by the power of the human spirit to transcend physical trappings. It was in the deepest squalor that I encountered the most spirited and spiritually evolved human beings. It was in this space that I reviewed the common notion of black ghettos as nothing but a breeding ground for hard-core criminals. In spite of reports of horrific forms of violent crime from colleagues, friends and members of the community seeking counselling, it was here that I met and interacted with some of the most beautiful human beings on earth.

Agisanang Domestic Abuse Prevention and Training (ADAPT) was conceived in 1992 following a research project that I undertook to examine the rate of identification of and attitudes towards battered women in health care settings. The completion of the study was followed by a process of consultation with the clinic management and members of the community, during which I shared the findings and recommendations of the study. The recommendations included setting up a counselling service for abused women.

It was during this process of consultation that I encountered a group of women leaders in Alexandra who questioned my motives for the research and proposed service. I was accused of being an academic and a researcher more interested in furthering her career than in the welfare of the people of Alexandra. Furthermore, I was not born and bred in Alex – an accusation that I heard levelled at many in the nine years that I spent in the community.

Here I was, a black woman who had just broken off from a previously white academic institution and from having to fight intense ideological battles, driven by a passion to engage in community-based research, having to answer to black women who asked me: Why Alex? Why not consider setting up such a service in Mabopane, your resident township? This challenged my sense of belonging in two worlds, the world of academia, dominated by white women, and that of grassroots, community-based activism, dominated by black women. Hurt, disappointed and almost discouraged, I crawled back to base to lick my wounds and process my feelings. There is a famous phrase in Sepedi: *"Go chechela morago ga se so tshaba, ke go tsea maatla"*. That is precisely what I did. I reflected a lot about leadership, and the qualities, roles and responsibilities of a good leader. Does leadership entail making decisions for others? If so, what criteria do we use to make such decisions? What tools should we employ to ensure that the outcome is in the best interest of the greatest number of people?

The women with whom I met were not necessarily the direct beneficiaries of the proposed service. I say this with caution, however, because domestic violence is not only the lot of the unemployed and the poor. Indeed, some of the very women with whom I met may, just like me, have been subjected to violence in their lives. During the course of my work in this field I have encountered prominent women who have suffered in silence and lived their private lives at the mercy of their abusers, who were respected business, political and community leaders.

After a week of reflection, I phoned and asked for a follow-up meeting with the group. I went back driven by a resurgence of energy and a determination that I could not explain rationally. I wanted them to tell me to my face that I was not allowed in the community and that they, as representatives of the community, did not approve the establishment of the proposed service. I went back with a sense that although I might not have been born and bred in Alexandra, I could claim any township as my home. At our meeting I was not given either a clear green light or a red no-go sign, but something in between.

In the years that I spent in the community, I persevered in my attempts to involve some of these prominent women leaders in my work. Painful and strenuous as that perseverance proved to be, I used the experience as an opportunity to learn the art of turning my enemies into allies. As with other battles, this one was never fully won. In spite of my attempts to involve these women in my programme, some never set foot in my office, let alone organised a meeting to discuss how we could collectively confront violence against women in the community.

So, while I had expected my most hostile response to come from men, it was from women that I received tacit disapproval and attempted sabotage. Without resorting to the simplistic and biased perception of women being their own worst enemy, I recognise and have experienced gender transformation as a deeply personal and sometimes painful journey. As we move on in our attempts to change gender roles and attitudes, I suggest that the conscientisation of men should be accompanied by women's honest reflections on the possibilities of moving beyond the personal to a much deeper understanding of revolutionary feminism.

I started off in a small office at Alexandra Health and University Clinic, where I received wonderful support from David Robb and the rest of the clinic management. Just a few weeks after I had started, however, my office was broken into. In spite of burglar bars and security personnel on site, my computer, disks, including back-up disks that I had locked in the cupboard, were stolen. In just one night, all the data that I had accumulated over the years disappeared. I had bought the computer out of my own pocket, and hadn't the money to replace it.

I was feeling alone and was thinking of giving up and finding another job when a colleague, friend and revolutionary, Dr Dumo Baqwa, walked into my office, having heard about the break-in. In his usual, laid-back way he gave me a long lecture about resistance, internalised racism and the political economy of development in Africa. I use the word "lecture" deliberately because for the first time in any of our discussions about these matters, I didn't say a word. I simply hadn't the energy to respond, and he must have loved it. Those who knew Dumo will recall how he would take his time to make a point, occasionally interspersing his words with bursts of loud laughter. Dumo is no more; he too has been called to join the cadre of revolutionaries tasked with the attainment of spiritual liberation for Africa. And I did not leave. After that lecture, how could I have?

I worked in Alexandra for nine years, the longest I have ever been in one place. There were immense challenges along the way, and I would not have survived without my family. My mother, Boitumelo, sent packets of tomatoes and onions from Mabopane for the children and me. My father, Rantebo, took over the instalments on my little car. Kgalalelo, still in nappies, kept me company from her pram as I was setting up the office. There were times when I could not afford to buy her milk or juice, and all I could give her was a bottle of warm water before she went to sleep. Katlego loved me unconditionally throughout that period. My sister Lenyalo and my brothers Mosire, Manyane and Serake were the most wonderful co-parents that anyone could wish for. My brother-in-law, Lehlohonolo Moagi, supported me with office stationery and marketing, accompanying me to meetings with potential funders in the early and most challenging stages of the journey.

I could have changed jobs. I could have gone for a "secure" position with a good package, but I would not have learnt the lessons. I would not be who I am today. I have paid the price for sticking it out; my marriage crumbled and for a while I was a bitter and angry person. I also suffered immense financial strain over the years. The cost, however, has been more than outweighed by the reward of finding my purpose in life.

I was taught amazing lessons by various teachers, notably the black working-class women whom I encountered in Alexandra and beyond. I acknowledge with gratitude and respect the contribution they made in my life. I am particularly grateful to Lerato Masango and *Mme* MaMthethwa, who used to work in the nearby Alexandra Childminders' Project office, for their occasional gifts of R5 or R10 for petrol. There were women who bought food for my children whenever the going got tough. When I arrived in the community, *Mme* Beauty More was one of the women who supported ADAPT all the way in spite of immense challenges that she herself faced at Thusong Youth Centre. I cannot name all, but I was supported by many. I am who I am today because these women carried me. I truly rode on the shoulders of giants. I am visible today because they carried me high. I have grown because of having studied their philosophy of life. It took me some time; their philosophy is very simple, and for a while it proved incomprehensible to someone like me, already negatively affected by a Western education.

Beyond our northern borders I have worked with women in countries such as Zimbabwe, Kenya and Somalia. Somalia was a shock to my system. In 1997 I left South Africa for Mogadishu with a fellow trainer and friend, Penny Plowman, on a NOVIB assignment to facilitate gender training with specific focus on violence against women. We left Johannesburg, flying South African Airways to Nairobi, Kenya, arriving in the afternoon. We overnighted in Nairobi, with plans to proceed to Mogadishu the next day.

We boarded our Air Afrique flight around midday the next day. From the outside, the plane looked perfectly alright. Once inside, though, we were assaulted by a revolting smell from a dysfunctional air conditioning system. With my nostrils still adjusting to the environment, I noticed that even though we had seats allocated to us, everyone seemed to be sitting just anywhere. I later discovered that many of the seats were broken and some did not even have seat belts. Settling next to a window and looking out to see a British Airways jumbo jet on the runway next to us, I experienced a surge of resentment against all those British Airways passengers, sitting comfortably in their designated seats, and enjoying the air conditioning! Looking around me, I noticed that the business class section did not boast a single seat. Instead there were boxes, tied together to prevent them from shifting during the flight. Well, that's one consolation, I thought: we're all equal on this flight.

We finally reached our destination, without having heard the captain's voice even once. On our arrival, we were welcomed by our hostess, Faiza Mohamed, wearing one of the most beautiful smiles that I have ever seen. In a matter of minutes, I was wrapped up in her warmth and I found a safe haven in her big heart.

After our passports had been whisked away to be checked in a building that had obviously been blown up during the war, we drove into Mogadishu, accompanied by a convoy of trucks filled with young men carrying automatic weapons. Our entry into what had once been Mogadishu brought me face to face with the effects of war. Faiza pointed out heaps of rubble that had once been a hospital, a university, a hotel school. My country was only three years into the new dispensation and the road to peace was still slippery. Seeing the aftermath of war in Mogadishu made me think of South Africa and the impending civil war just before 1994. Suddenly, I was gripped with fear for my country.

The most painful part of my seven-day stay in Mogadishu involved listening to women's accounts of rape during war. At first they were reluctant to speak because they were not really aware of how widespread a phenomenon this was. In fact, many seemed to think that their experience of rape was unique. Once they started to open up and remove the veil covering their wounded hearts, words and tears flowed abundantly. They were deeply shocked to learn that other women had gone through similar experiences. As trainer and support group facilitator, I absorbed an enormous amount of pain in the last 48 hours of my stay in Mogadishu. When I returned home, I found myself immobilised by rage, pain and fear; unable to go on with my life and my work, I realised that I myself needed counselling.

Beyond the borders of Africa, I have interacted with the most civil and humble as well as the most arrogant Western women. These last considered themselves God's gift to women in Africa. Women in Africa have long been portrayed as helpless and apathetic victims, dependent on the wise intervention of their sisters in the developed world. Western women are well aware of injustices, racism and discrimination on their own doorsteps, yet instead of focusing first on addressing imbalances in their home countries and then making connections with what is happening globally, many have embraced the role of martyr and gone all out to save Africa.

When I addressed the Women's Health Conference in Toronto, Canada in 1996, I was struck by the fact that the native women appeared in the programme only to entertain guests with their songs, chants and poetry. This reminded me so much of the tourism industry here in South Africa, where, without owning any stake or shares in the operation, many indigenous people are used as entertainers to sing and dance for international tourists. Once again, our culture and our essence have become trivialised, reduced to an exotic type of entertainment or a form of prostitution. Visitors may enjoy watching a group of Zulus dancing around the fire, but do they truly appreciate this as an expression of culture? What most miss, with our permission of course, is that our culture, our songs, our dance and chants have a deep spiritual significance. The issue of cultural equity remains central to the reconciliation of all races and countries. As it is, acculturation is mainly unidirectional, with black people absorbing white culture, including its waste, while white people, assisted by digital and video cameras, continue in their role as owners and creators of images of black life.

It was disheartening to find that the conference programme failed to allocate time and space for women of the First Nations to speak out about their health situation. These women have a lot to share about the ancient and natural ways of healing that have been used by native medicine women and men. Instead of finding new ways of healing the planet, and in that way reducing some of the chronic diseases prevalent today, delegates devoted a great deal of time to modern technology and drugs used to treat conditions such as breast cancer. An honest interaction with the First Nations would have provided guidance and strengthened an argument for preventative medicine, thereby reducing health budgets and saving us time and the stress that comes with high-tech medicine.

In similar vein, a visit I made to Australia brought to my attention the depth and extent of the harm done to Aboriginal communities. South Africa was then at the beginning of the transformation process and received endless delegations from Australia to assist with reconciliation and transformation. At the time of the Australian delegations to South Africa, the Aboriginal Health Council of South Australia and the Dulwich Centre were involved in the Reclaiming Our Stories,

Reclaiming Our Lives project, which was guided by the philosophy that it was not for people outside the Aboriginal community to provide answers. The project called instead for complete honouring of and respect for the special knowledge and skills relating to healing that Aboriginal communities already possess. The project faced problems such as the increasing prevalence of deaths of Aboriginal people in custody as well as their lack of access to mainstream services. I could not help but wonder what these experts could possibly teach us about integration and reconciliation when they had left their real experts behind in their own back yard.

The lie that the North is the saviour and rescuer of indigenous communities of the South has been perpetuated for too long, and must come to an end. All international powerhouses, from the United States, the United Nations and NATO to the Commonwealth and the European Union must take their public pronouncements and rhetoric back home. After all, true leaders lead and teach by example. The world has had enough war, violence, poverty and spiritual displacement.

My encounter with women in Europe has been a source of both intense exhilaration and rage. I have fond memories of a trip to Ireland in 1992, where I was made welcome from Cork through to Dublin, from Belfast to Derry. I spent time with various women's groups, amazed at our sameness in spite of our different racial origins. My skin was darker than theirs, and that made me different, yet politically we had so much to share. I felt with them on hearing accounts of strip-searching by British security officials in Irish and British jails in an attempt to degrade and humiliate women political prisoners. I was told of a woman who was held down by eight security officials and stripped while she was having her period. Her sanitary pad was taken away to be inspected by the so-called medic. Her vagina was opened and looked into. To strip-search a woman who is menstruating and take her blood away for inspection is a despicable act. That these officials were willing participants in such a vile and extreme expression of hatred for womanhood speaks volumes about them. It says that they were as imprisoned and displaced as those they were meant to keep behind bars.

After working hard during rallies, conferences and seminars in many countries, I have joined with women in playing hard too. I have spent some unforgettable moments with women in pubs around the world. I don't drink; I have thankfully learnt both how to access my chaotic fire and how to relax without resorting to addictive substances. Yet I am most concerned about the increasing number of women who are crumbling under the might and power of alcohol and drugs. Using the women's liberation ticket, tobacco and liquor companies have refined their advertising to target women. Already toiling beneath the other burdens that they have to carry, an increasing number of women suffer from psychosomatic and alcohol-related illnesses.

We should not shy away from acknowledging the physical toll that working in the field of women's empowerment and gender transformation takes on us. In her book, *Women's Bodies, Women's Wisdom*[7], Dr Christiane Northrup urges women to become more open and conscious of the ways in which they contribute to the negative patriarchal loop. As we become more conscious of our contribution to an addictive society, we will be empowered to improve our health as individuals

[7] *Op. cit.*

and as a society. An empowerment that does not guarantee complete physical, psychological, economic and spiritual health will do nothing for either us or the planet.

Be that as it may, some of my most remarkable experiences with women around the globe have been in discotheques and pubs. Have you ever been in a pub where there is a bunch of happy women laughing out loud in one corner? Have you noticed the irritation on men's faces as they looked their way? Happy and centred women are threatening to some men. It is no wonder that governments across the globe are involved with overt and covert operations aimed at keeping women burdened, unhappy and miserable. The black consciousness philosophy posed a threat simply because it called for self-love and self-pride. Revolutionary feminism calls for those very same things.

I have had the most intimate and explosive discussions about sex and sexuality in the company of women across the globe. I remember that on one occasion in Dublin, one of the women in the group, who was a writer and much older than most of us, said that she could never imagine herself being seduced by another woman. A woman of the same age, also a writer and a poet, challenged her and shared her experiences of how society had viewed her as a woman and a lesbian. It was a truly amazing experience for me, a young black heterosexual woman from Africa, to be among older, white, free-spirited women talking about sex in a country known for its conservative views on abortion.

On some occasions, discussions about sex have led to a questioning of the commonly held belief that size matters. Subscription to this belief reinforces the phallocentric view of masculinity that says a man is a man not because he provides for his family, but because he has a penis. In *Black Looks*[8], bell hooks traces this shift from patriarchy, the capacity to assert power over others, to phallocentrism, where the focus became the penis. What the man does with his penis and where, she explains, became a way to assert his masculinity. As a result, a man who was defined sexually and who believed in the domination and sexual possession of women became the norm. Instead of focusing on other aspects of their humanity, men defined their manhood by their sexual conquests. The issue of male sexual conquest and the size of a man's penis is but a step away from a racist view of manhood and masculinity. Unfortunately, as a society, we have bought into this view. Journalistic and other reports on fatherhood tend to portray white fathers as providers who are also capable of giving and receiving love, while black men are portrayed as sex maniacs and drunks. As a community, we are collectively charged with the responsibility of changing representations of black masculinity. There is so much more to a black man than the size of his penis.

In our quest to denounce racist and sexist violence in both intimate and international relations, we are challenged to erase a masculine script that is devoid of compassion and is directed by the pleasure derived from imposing one's will on another through fear and force. Just as important, we need to reject the internalised image of the black man as a caged, sexually indiscriminate half-naked savage, his ebony body shining with sweat and rippling with muscles acquired through years of hard exploitative labour.

Furthermore, an undue focus on a man's penis raises questions about women's ability to take full

[8] Hooks, B. 1992. *Black Looks: Race and Representation*. Boston, MA: South End Press.

responsibility for their own pleasure rather than putting immense pressure on men. It also raises questions about women's willingness and ability to experience the fullness of sex without penetration by a man.

Many straight women will tell you of a sexual experience with a well-endowed but egotistical man, unable even to spell the word "love" and driven purely by the desire to conquer and invade as many women's bodies as possible. A conqueror such as this is excited not by the pleasure of sex, but by overcoming women's resistance and imposing his male power on them. For a woman, such an encounter is nothing more than a repulsive invasion. However, these women can probably also tell of a sexual encounter with a less well-endowed man whose delightful, unhurried and focused attention to detail was completely unselfish. Similarly, sexually liberated straight women and lesbians can tell of the most exquisite sexual experience without penetration by a partner. There is more to a woman's body than tits, pussy and a butt, yet aided by contemporary fashion and representations of the female body in popular culture, the male gaze is steered to view certain body parts as representative of heightened sexuality. Increasingly, the female body is defined as desirable and beautiful (and hot) when it is "sexually free", meaning willing to succumb to male lust.

Women's notions of good sex as being sex in which they are dominated by men are rooted in patriarchal sexual beliefs. Since growing up in such a society predisposes women to abuse, many come to sexual relations wounded. Yet the socialisation of men to claim the right to domination and conquest and to demand that women be submissive creates conflict within both women and men. Teaching boys to view tenderness as a sign of weakness and encouraging men to maintain their dominant sexual power at all cost will breed not only emotional disconnection but sexual dysfunction as well.

As a way of reconnecting to our deeper selves and healing current gender relations, we need to renegotiate what it means to be women and men and, ultimately, what it means to be human. After all, women and men as a group each make up half of humanity. To become whole, we are called to live our lives fully and free from current cultural prescriptions sold to us as a liberated sexuality.

I had been celibate by choice for almost two years when I rediscovered the depth and intensity of sex. Ironically, it was not with a partner that I rediscovered sex. Such deep and intense feelings were the result of having found my centred inner feminine. Never had I felt more internally and profoundly sensuous than at that time. It was such a beautiful feeling; I carried it in me and enjoyed it to the fullest. What was even more intriguing about it was that it was for my exclusive enjoyment and I guarded it jealously. I did not feel that I needed to use it to lure a man to my bed. I was happy to live consciously with a part of me that I had never really got to know well before. I found my depth and my ability to love. I also gave myself permission to receive love.

Receiving love and believing that you are deserving of what you are receiving is closely correlated with our sense of self and our motive for giving. In its pure form, giving should give us joy not because we are one up, but because we expect nothing in return. In its impure form, giving is bound up with power and the belief that we are doing someone a favour. Similarly, receiving with arrogance is nothing more than giving expression to a sense of entitlement. How much better to receive with humility and gratitude, yet at the same time acknowledge that you are worthy of what you receive.

The purity, depth and quality of our sexual relationships is closely dependent on our ability to give and receive love, which, in turn, is closely tied to our self-worth and personal liberation. Part of our liberation will come from healing our sexual wounds. Once healed, we will no longer view and use other people (women or men) as sexual objects.

When I started to work in the field of gender relations, in which I have been both a teacher and a student for so many years, I was driven largely by pain, anger and bitterness. I have, over time, matured as a person and as an activist. I have been afforded endless opportunities to confront my inadequacies and learn the art of self-analysis and self-care. I am healing.

I ventured out to fix the world, yet I have come to learn that this mission will be accomplished only when we all realise that the world cannot change unless we focus on changing ourselves. In my work, I taught all about the importance of taking care of our bodies, minds and soul, while I myself was incapable of doing so. I was eloquent, articulate, and very convincing. I probably left people wishing they could be like me. Little did they know that I was not really practising what I was preaching. I implored women to take care of themselves, to be gentle and loving to their bodies and their soul, while I was an addict, addicted to my work. It is true what they say; we teach what we need to learn most.

A turning point came one Saturday, after I had I spent the day addressing one gathering after another, my last engagement being the facilitation of a workshop on family and relationship enrichment in a church in the centre of Johannesburg. I left the workshop in the evening to go home to a cold, unlit house. My children were on holiday, staying with my parents. I was out giving light while my own home was dark. I lashed out at my ancestors, castigating them for making me work so hard helping people to rebuild their homes while I did not have anyone to come home to. I cried myself to sleep.

The next day I had to prepare to leave for Atlanta to attend the National Black Women's Health Project Conference. When I arrived at my hotel, I was greeted with a most beautiful sight; black women wherever I looked. It had been some time since I had seen so much beauty all under one roof. The walls were covered with African textiles and masks; I felt so at home. I will never forget the electrifying energy shared by Sweet Honey and the Rock in the evening, or the pleasure and honour of working with Bylle Avery, Ama Saran and Barbara Love, and of meeting bell hooks and Angela Davis.

Throughout the conference, I specifically chose to participate in breakaway sessions that had something to do with self-care. In the sessions, we analysed how we live our working lives in ways that adversely affect our physical, mental and spiritual health. We deliberated on the importance of creating circles of love in our lives rather than feeling a sense of entitlement and expecting to receive love in exchange for our work. We recognised how we tend to rescue others while we ourselves have difficulty with being rescued. Much of what was said resonated immediately, while some of it did not really hit home until I had burned most of my fingers. After all, experience is the best teacher. *Thutokgolo e tswa lebading.* It is only when you have dealt with ego that you find meaningful healing. From where I stand in my life now, I strongly advocate including self-analysis and self-care as integral parts of any gender instruction and training.

During my tenure as founder and director of ADAPT, I developed an empowerment model that views the woman as the binding force that holds family and community life together. The model recognises that the woman who is abused does not exist in isolation, and that her healing is closely tied to the healing of her partner, her family and the community. Further, the model recognises that violence against women is about male power and that the key to ending this crime lies in addressing power imbalances between women and men in all sectors. It is from such an understanding that I developed and introduced a programme geared toward supporting men in their journey to a place of healing, and it is from that experience that I would like to pay tribute to the following men:

Mike Sithe

Thank you for sharing your life story. You have, in your young life, faced immense challenges, including displacement from your home as a result of political violence. In spite of all you have been through, you remain eager: eager to learn to live a life, eager to strive for nothing but the best and overcome challenges.

I have a picture of you with your beautiful daughter. You are a wonderful, caring, young black father. I know you have limited financial means to care for her adequately. I know, too, that you have unlimited love for her. Keep on striving for nothing but the best. You deserve the best because you are the best.

Nhlanhla Mabizela

What do I say about you? Humble, with a subdued, naughty smile and a twinkle in your eye. You are a leader. You often lead without being aware of your capabilities or even believing in the magnitude of the role that you are destined to play on this planet. I remember you in one of our conflict-ridden group meetings. I remember how hurt you were; I remember the things you said. You threatened to leave the men's group because you did not want to associate yourself with any negativity. Deep down, I knew that you would not quit. You are the type of man who never gives up on himself.

Innocent Toto

"Deep" is the word that comes to mind when I think of you. There is so much more to you than meets the eye. You, like most young black men, had a difficult childhood. You are steady and quiet, a man of few words. You remind me so much of my father, who is a deeply sensitive and feeling human being. Living in a society that does not have much room for men who can feel can be very alienating and painful. A feeling man, that's what you are.

Boitshepo Lesetedi

In the time that we worked (and laughed and fought) together, I have seen you evolve as an activist, a father and a husband. The transition has not been easy, but I have seen you open up like a rose facing the sun after the rain. I have seen you rise up, taking responsibility for your actions, including confronting me head-on for my imperfections and inconsistencies. Keep on keeping on, my dear brother.

Prince Masina

It is hard to imagine such a gentle soul behind bars for armed robbery. In my first encounter with you at Leeuwkop Prison when we came to facilitate a workshop on male violence, you stood out – was it your height, or your neat prison uniform, or the light in your eyes?

You were active in the prison project while you were behind bars. Once released you became a part of ADAPT and went back to prison with us to continue where you left off whilst still inside. You have been through so much in your life; you have overcome so many obstacles. Don't let the final tests break you. You cannot give up now, or at any other time, for that matter. I pray to the Goddess that one day we will find a way of keeping black men in their communities instead of sending them back to prison over and over again.

Pule Mosenohi

The first time I met you was when we interviewed you for the men's counselling training programme. We asked everyone the same question: when last did you hit a woman? Many told lies, many told the truth reluctantly. You told the truth without any hesitation.

I have watched you evolve as a father to your girls despite serious financial constraints and unemployment. You forced us, a women's organisation, to organise our meetings in such a way that we accommodated you as a father. To hear you remind us to make time for you to pick up your daughter from pre-school was a wake-up call. We women tend to think that we are the ones who are gender sensitive, yet we continue to relate to men in ways that contradict that. Thank you for being our teacher.

Samukelo Madonsela

One thing I remember about you is your laughter – you spent so many of your working hours laughing. I know how much pressure you were under. When you joined us, you were literally thrown in at the deep end. When you lost so many of your family members and loved ones in a short space of time, I was afraid for you. The pain was etched into your face and I heard it in your voice. Yet, you triumphed. I remember with fondness and warmth the things you said about your father just before he died. With such a bond, he will always be by your side. May you be guided in your work and in your life.

Sello Maake kaNcube

How do I thank you for what you did for ADAPT? All the minutes, hours, days and months; the knowledge and life experience that you shared with young men without asking for much in return. You have contributed to a foundation, which I hope and pray will strengthen black men's ability to live with compassion. As an actor, you taught us that we are all actors and that life is a stage. At a personal level, you have contributed to my growth. Thank you.

Finally, I would like to thank all the men who have worked with me at various places and times. I would like to thank them specifically for restoring my faith in men. If I lose faith in men, I lose faith in myself. My liberation as a black person and a woman is closely tied to the liberation of black people and men.

Yes, I was the one to found ADAPT, but its success over the years arose from an eternal spring of love and support from my family, members of staff, volunteers and the community, and the financial support of many local and international donors. My departure from the organisation on 25 November 2000, International Day of No Violence Against Women, was marked by an ancestral celebration led by our elders, *badimo ba ba jang bogobe*, to mark a return to indigenous teachings. The restoration of human dignity will emanate from the healing of the body, mind and spirit. The time for Africa's healing is Now.

Afrika Wee! Bana ba mmala wa mosidi wa pitsana.
Bana ba moritshana mofitlha botlhale go tswa Lowe.
Ahaa! Afrika, nako ke yona.

Hearing voices

It is Friday, 16 June 2000 and I am at Oslo airport amidst a sea of white faces, waiting for a British Airways flight home via Heathrow. The chance of seeing someone of African descent in this busy airport on this day seems as remote as the possibility of snow in Musina. I have just spent some days in Oslo, where, with Dr Tom Andersen, a world-renowned family therapist, I delivered a keynote address at the annual World Family Therapy Congress.

To share the stage with him was more than an honour. In addition to reading some of his publications when I was a postgraduate psychology student, I had also read so much about him. On the Wednesday, before the opening, I had a sense that something magical was about to happen. I spent some time in conversation with my ancestors before leaving first for breakfast, then for the conference venue. I did not really know what to expect. There was a part of me that was afraid; there was another part that knew that everything would be perfectly okay.

I met Tom Andersen for breakfast. A very gentle and humble Norwegian, he confessed to me that he was anxious. I lied and said I was not, and invited him to draw from my energy. We laughed over that. As we chatted, he spoke about our differences: the fact that he was white and I was black, that he was from the North and I from the South, that he was a man and I a woman, that he belonged to the oppressor's culture, and I came from the oppressed – yet for all that, we had our humanity in common, and we come from One source. The moment called for a celebration of both our sameness and diversity.

Tom mentioned that in his presentation, he would read from Martin Luther King, Nelson Mandela, the Norwegian Inge Eidsvag and Harry Goolishan, the Armenian American psychiatrist, all of whom have called for a rejection of violence and war as a way of solving conflict. Their message serves as inspiration to all people of the world to create a language of love that has no room for revenge or hatred. For this to happen, the world has to reject the power that feeds and survives on the denial and suppression of other people's power.

For me, that translated into an acknowledgement that the current global language of invasion, occupation, violence, terrorism, hunger, deprivation and death perpetuates our collective hatred and self-destruction. As citizens of the world, we are creative agents, and we can reframe and begin to speak a language of reconciliation.

However, reconciliation does not just happen. Like self-respect, it needs patience and determination. It feeds on consistency, integrity and dignity. It involves far more than recommendations from the head, as prescribed in endless cease-fire resolutions. For reconciliation to occur, the heart has to be involved. It is from the heart that both the oppressed and oppressor can let go of a devastating past based on the illusion of superiority and face a future based on the reality of peaceful co-existence and interdependence. It is with the strength that comes from the heart that we can all save ourselves from drowning in a sea of apathy and despair. It is from our heart of hearts that we can open ourselves to the miracle of forgiveness.

Forgiveness does not mean that we should condone or even try to forget our despicable past. For black South Africans, proving that we have healed and that we can forgive does not mean we should pretend that the injustices of the past did not happen. Forgiveness is an attempt to liberate our hearts from the weight of hatred and the quest for revenge. Rather than being an act of weak surrender, forgiveness can become a means to reclaim our power and freedom from a yesterday that has kept us captive for decades. Ultimately, we can open up to our present, but we do not have to forget our yesterday.

I am today
I want to be tomorrow
I was yesterday
How can I be today
without my yesterday?
What would I become
without my today?

Bring back my yesterday
Plain and simple
How dare you
label it baggage
Who are you
to prescribe forgiveness
and demand forgetfulness?

Bring back my yesterday
Let me take my time
as I slowly sift it like sand
one grain after another.

Let me eventually carry it
not like a rock in my heart
but as a jewel in my soul.
In time
My time.

How can I be
Without I am
How can there be I am
Without I was
It's my story
My roots
My suffering
My joy
It is my life.

Forgive and forget
What a damn cheek
I will forgive eventually
But I will never
Forget my yesterday.

After our breakfast, Tom and I made our way to the
conference venue, which held more than 1 600 people. I
remember very vividly the thoughts and feelings that
rushed through me as I sat down on the stage facing the
multitude. The effects of being raised in apartheid South
Africa came surging back, as I scanned the ocean of white
faces in search of a sprinkle of black faces from outside
Europe. I saw white and black first, and human second.
To lift myself above my instinctive response, I mentally
turned to the wisdom of Maya Angelou, which I keep
stored inside my head – moving beyond the skin into the

true heart of being, we are more alike than unlike. At that moment, I smelled freedom.

The venue was beautifully decorated with foliage, fruit and flowers. It crackled with energy; there was a glow on people's faces. Everywhere around me people were kissing, smiling and hugging. I had the honour of meeting Giofranco Cecchin, yet another world leader on family therapy living in Milan.

The opening ceremony commenced with choir members in Norwegian national dress singing a song titled "Welcome to Norway". We were informed later that the choir members were all doctors, nurses and patients. Breaking down the barriers between professionals and patients, I thought. Western medicine has been hampered by the notion that doctors, nurses and other health care professionals are the experts, and patients the passive recipients of health care. Yet the will to health and healing belongs to individuals. Even with the most advanced medical technology, unless patients have the will to live, doctors cannot heal. Western medical science would take a great step forward if only it would open itself to the wisdom of the heart, mind and soul.

Tom and I were introduced. I cannot recall the exact words used, but I seem to remember being described as a healer, and an aspiring writer living in both Johannesburg and a rural village in South Africa. We were called forward. Because of my appearance and my size, my small frame and my unstraightened African hair partially covered by a head wrap, many of the participants wondered whether I was up to the task. One grey-haired white male psychiatrist from London confessed during the tea break that he thought I had been set up.

Following the address, I felt like an actor who has just won a coveted award. The love and appreciation that poured from the participants from the South affirmed me. The delegates from Africa, Asia and Latin America claimed my voice as their own. This humbling experience reminded me of the words of Martin Carter, the Guyanese poet who describes the wretched people of the earth as people who do not sleep to dream but dream to change the world. To have the opportunity to tell our own stories about the indigenous wisdom and healing powers of our forefathers and foremothers to an audience in Europe was, for me, part of a broader revolutionary struggle for Africa's emancipation.

For decades, the worth of an African as a visionary and leader has been assessed in terms of whether she or he studied at Harvard, Columbia, Oxford, Cambridge or another leading institution of the West. To be awarded an international scholarship such as a Rhodes or Fullbright scholarship has always been perceived as highly prestigious. The great Western institutions unquestionably played an enormous role in creating a cadre of outstanding leaders in the 20th century. In this, the 21st century, however, the agenda for personal and global development will change. While Africa has always been perceived as the dark continent, in this new era, the continent shall now be proclaimed a place of freedom, abundance and peace. Now is the time for scholars in the West to seek scholarships to learn from Africans the art of returning humanity to humans. In the words of Steve Biko: "We believe that in the long run the special contribution to the world by Africa will be in this field of human relationship. The great powers of the world may have done wonders in giving the world an industrial and military look, but the great gift still has to come from Africa – giving the world a more human face".[9] It takes the most oppressed, the poorest of the poor and those who have suffered extreme physical and psychological battering to teach the lessons of nobility and freedom, spiritual wealth and abundance, love and peace. Africa is being prepared to lead the world.

On the Thursday evening we were treated to a delightful jam session. I was thrilled to discover that the conference participants, most of whom were health workers, could also play a variety of musical instruments. My attention was drawn to a psychiatrist from London, who was playing the saxophone, and who introduced himself as "Bentovin". Of all the instruments, a saxophone has always fascinated me, and, as I have already confessed, there was a time when I hoped to learn to play. However, I was told that the sax is difficult, and you need strong lungs to blow it. I shared my unrealised dream with my new-found friend, who assured me that there is nothing hard about playing the saxophone; all you need is discipline.

Discipline. A lot of creativity comes out of discipline. Some would say that even more creativity comes out of chaos, but personally, I wouldn't mind a bit of both. The duality of life – Africa and Europe, white and black, young and old, masculine and feminine, yin and yang.

I know with great certainty that I always have a guardian angel walking before me, beside me and behind me. However, it took me a while to hear the voices. It is all part of the journey.

I have always known that we all interface with sacred energies that are larger than us, yet not visible to the naked eye. Despite knowing this, I have faltered in

[9] Biko, S. 1996. *I Write What I Like: A Selection of his Writings*. Johannesburg: Ravan Press: p.47.

finding and sticking to the path. It is all part of the journey.

With unconditional love and guidance from the Creative Creator, I am a willing student of life. There is no other way.

Running a marathon

It is 15 November 1996.

I am on board a South African Airways flight to New York. I do not enjoy flying; my hands get sweaty when the flight gets bumpy. This is my fifth overseas trip this year. My first trip was in February, when I went to Geneva, Switzerland for a World Health Organization consultative meeting. A few weeks later I went to Holland to present a paper on the position of South African women at the South African Embassy in The Hague. In June I was in Toronto, Canada as one of the keynote speakers at the Women's Health Conference, after which I travelled to Washington DC and San Francisco for an advocacy and lobbying workshop in September. And now, only six weeks later, I am on my way to New York and Los Angeles to receive an international human rights award.

If I am not flying overseas, it is not unusual for me to be at the airport by half past five in the morning to catch the first flight to Cape Town, Durban, Port Elizabeth or some other destination in Southern Africa. If I am not flying, I am in a car driving somewhere. I am constantly in motion. Will this race ever end?

I feel a strong need to sit quietly and listen to the whispers in my heart. Strangely though, the very thought of being still sends me racing as far away from myself as possible, even though deep down I know that the whispers will ultimately become rumblings that will erupt like a volcano. Yet I still think I can outrun the mudslide.

The journey to where I am has been a long and eventful one, in which my marriage and subsequent divorce have been significant turning points. Looking back, I am beginning to realise that marriage is no trifling matter. So many of us get married without taking the time to reflect on the institution – its rules, our roles, and the games we play because there is a difference between who we really are and what society expects of us. When I look back, I still feel residual pain. As I look closely, though, I see glimpses of my life's purpose emerging. I am on a journey to healing.

As a traveller, I wonder: would I be able to provide signposts for others embarking on this journey if I had not been on that road myself? At the time of my preparation, I was the most miserable person on earth. Life was not worth living. I even tried to commit suicide when I was pregnant with my daughter. After taking an overdose of medication I slept for two days. No-one knew and no-one noticed because I was alone for the weekend. Nothing happened, it was not meant to be. My beautiful bouncing baby girl was born healthy, and she has been full of life ever since.

My son, who was five at the time, witnessed this heartbreaking and yet soul-strengthening rite of passage. He took in my pain; it affected and infected his innocent and pure soul. It was only later that he confided in me, telling me that he always knew what I was going through despite my attempts to hide my pain from him. He later told me that there were nights when he had to sleep under his bed, covering his head with a pillow because he could not deal with my muffled sobs. I had a sense that it had affected him, but I did not really know how much until we spoke about it recently, now that he is a teenager. It came as a shock to learn that he had also contemplated taking his life. I am so grateful for the opportunity to reconstruct my relationship with him. He loves me and I love him, and that is all we need to heal our wounds.

Now that I am on my way to that special destination, I realise that my purpose in life is to accompany women and men to a place of healing. This feels very much like waiting at the side of the road providing energy drinks to marathon runners as they pass through. I don't make them want to run the marathon; they make that decision themselves. I don't determine their pace; that depends on their inner strength and determination. All that is required of me is to offer a drink that will quench their thirst and provide energy for what may seem like a never-ending race.

For many of us, pain has been a long-standing feature of our lives. For some, there is still no visible guiding light ahead. Many of us think that we will never make it to the finishing line. Whether we get there running, walking, crawling, or carried by fellow runners, the point is that we will have made it – but that won't be the end. You see, we live our lives in such a way that when we get to a point of victory, goalposts are shifted. This race is never fully completed. If we are brave enough to grow, we will continue to run, walk, crawl or fall down, only to get up and start all over again. We will grow in spite of the pain.

Pain is a necessary condition for our joy. If we cannot and do not experience sorrow at some point in our lives, we will never get to know what joy feels like; we will not achieve the enlightenment necessary to feel the beauty within. We will neither experience inner peace nor hear the inner voice.

I feel the deepest gratitude to my ancestors for throwing me in the deep end, but at the same time loving me enough to make it possible for me to pass these difficult tests of life. If I have given the impression so far that I passed all the tests, that certainly isn't the case. I have failed many. I have on many occasions beaten up on myself for being a "failure", not realising that failure can signify progress, depending on how you look at your path.

In this life, there is no success or failure; there are lessons. Every lesson offers profound insights acquired through moments of spiritual wakefulness and humility. The participants in life's race aren't divided into winners and losers; all the runners are gold medal material. All the medals are gold; there is no silver or bronze. We are all good enough.

I am on my way to receive an international human rights award. I could not have done it on my own. There were any number of people along the way providing me with energy drinks, and many others cheered me on. Yet others carried me when I could not go on. Even though I am the one to receive a gold medal, the credit goes to all those who affect and are affected by my existence. I am blessed.

It is the end of 2001.

There is a saying in my language: *"Tshipo o rile ke lebelo, motlhaba wa re ke namile"*. I always knew in my inmost heart that I could not ignore my calling, but I still thought I was smart enough. Mother Nature has caught up with me; otherwise I would not be writing this book. My life came to a standstill in 2000; it was time to respond fully to my ancestral calling.

One morning in March 2000 I got up in tears, confused, with my soul on fire. Packing my bag, not knowing where I was heading, I left my baby crying in the arms of a child minder and my two older children at school, and went in search of a place where Soul resides. With not much money in my purse, driving a van that was not just a gas guzzler but unreliable to boot, I headed east.

It was six in the evening when I finally found myself at God's Window in Mpumalanga. My grandmother's spirit forced me to look down into the valley and insisted that I say the family praise. I was alone, confused, scared, wanting to die or disappear in the valley. I tried my grandmother's praise and I could not remember all of it. I ran away from the power towards my car. My grandmother insisted that I recall the praise overnight and come back before sunrise.

I had no idea where I was going to sleep. I drove back to Graskop and found a little hut in which to spend the night. I had a supper of soup and two slices of brown bread, as that was all I could afford. I spent the entire night recalling and memorising the praise and writing. By dawn, I was at the top of the mountain saying the praise, all of it. I made it. At that moment I heard a woman beating a drum somewhere below me, and I cried with joy. All alone, I danced. I was no longer afraid of the mountain. Unlike the previous evening, I walked around with no fear. I was embraced by my grandmother's love. A little while later I went down the hill and bought the drum. With the little money I had left I filled up with petrol, then phoned my family to let them know that I was alive and that I was on my way to Dikebu to the One who is a source of light on my path, my aunt *Mme* Kubele Motsei *Beetsi* Motaung.

Returning via the steep and winding roads in the Pilgrim's Rest district, I could not believe that I had driven safely to my destination the previous day, in a vehicle that was all but unroadworthy. I arrived in Dikebu at dusk. My aunt, my mother and my father were waiting for me. I broke down and knelt next to my aunt, humbling myself to the power of my ancestors. She did not say much, but took me in her arms. This time I could not even think about running. All I could do was surrender; it was time.

I was reminded of what Clarissa Pinkola Estés in her book, *Women who Run with the Wolves*, says about coming home: "When a woman is too long gone from home, she is less and less able to propel herself forward in life ... She's so cross-eyed with tiredness she trudges right on past the place of help and comfort ... Such a woman becomes pale yet contentious, more and more uncompromising, yet scattered. Her fuse burns shorter and shorter. Popular culture calls it "burn-out" – but it's more than that, it's *hambre del alma*, the starving soul".[10]

I read this several years ago. Now ask yourself; if I read it then, why did it take me so long to "get it"? Quite simply, I was afraid. I still am, sometimes. I cannot believe that I have survived in a perpetual spiritual deficit, making all kinds of excuses simply because I was afraid of sitting still and paying attention. Over time, the signals became so loud that it was impossible to dismiss, fight or run away from them.

Once I came home to myself, my spiritual journey started in earnest. Always accompanied by elders, my

[10] Pinkola Estés, C. 1992. *Women who Run with the Wolves*. London: Rider Books: p.279.

ancestral pilgrimage took me to various sacred places. We went to Mosi oa Thunya on the mighty Zambezi River in Zimbabwe, later taking a walk into Zambia at sunrise. We went to Modimolle in Limpopo, to Augrabies Falls in the Northern Cape, and to Robben Island, accompanied by the spirit of Makana. Our pilgrimage took us to Mount Kilimanjaro in Tanzania (where my elders came face to face with the primordial snake Rakgolo wa Madiba), the Suez Canal, the river Nile in Cairo and the mouth of Limpopo in Zongweni, Mozambique.

After driving for the entire day searching for the mouth of the Limpopo and finding it only in the evening, we encountered Senakangwedi, the firefly – our guiding light. I am always accompanied; I will always be guided. Even when I switched off the light after writing the first pages of this book in Limpopo, Senakangwedi came to my window, glowing in the dark. Falling asleep with a smile on my face, I knew that I was on the right track.

As I write this tonight, I am humbled into submission, my soul drifting into an ancestral chant led by Zim Nqgawana in his song "Umthandazo". Vacillating between a state of calm and chaos, I am thrown off balance by Ingebrigt Haker Flaten as he bellows through a contrabass. Bringing me back to my senses, Lefifi Tladi whispers in my ear. As I curl into the foetal position, Zim returns to sing me a lullaby, joined later by Andile Yenana.

It is the end of 2001 and I have not been in an aeroplane even once. I feel like a bird that has come home to its nest. From now on, I want to learn to work less and live better.

I thank my aunt, *Mme* Kubele, for her unconditional love and support, and for showing me the way back to the Source.

Moradi wa ba RaMotsei a Manyane, kgadi seikgantshi sa boNkoto, Khumi, Madumo le Serake sa boNtebo wa bo pheleu e boko bogolo Rantebo. Ke mogobyane ke tletse, bankgelli ba ntla ka dithoko, ba tshaba ge nka phamola motho ka mo tsenya bodibeng ba boSerake le Nkoto.

My grandmother Mmatshilo has always been a powerful part of my life, in both her physical and spiritual existence.

Ke Matshilo ngwana wa ba Moloisane, moana kgomo kgama. Ke mosetsana senyelosa matoporo a Ramotsei a Manyane le lerothodi Kubele sekgethwa ke banyeledi kgobo kgobo. Mosala gae ke mang? Ke segodisa lerothodi motlhola malatlha marapo masupa malwetse. Ke Matshilo mosetsana pelo sekgethwa, ke motho bathong, mathateng le thabong.

Ke sefataki, mma-mabele mabelega batho, mmopo mairwa phaleshe bogobe bafseng. Ke motho motlhompheng wena le nna go tshwana tshwane. Mosadimogolo pelo tumelo setlhola dibataka tswela pele. Mma Matoporo. Dibeetsi. Ditlogolo. Kubele lerothodi. Mokgonyana lerothodi.

I would not have survived without my beloved paternal grandfather, Ramoloi James Mosire Motsei. Even after passing on, he remains my unconditional love teacher and a model of the positive masculine. He was a gentle but firm and proud black man. I haven't a single memory of him speaking with a raised voice or with a face twisted in anger. I will always remember him with love.

The ancestral spirits of all whose blood run through my veins, Boo Ramotsei, Moloisane, Tladi, and Setshedi will always guide me. I am forever anchored by the love that flows from my great-great-grandfather, Poo Ramokolokolo Manyane, who left Lehurutshe to avoid a war, and settled in Mosetlha. It is for this reason that I remain *Mohurutshe tlholegong, Mokgatla kgodisong.* Without the love and care of my ancestors, what would I have become?

A return to Mapulaneng Hospital

I left Masana Hospital (now Mapulaneng) in Bushbuckridge in 1981 as a newly qualified young nurse. I had first come to Bushbuckridge after matriculating from Hebron High School. At 17, I did not feel eager to plunge into tertiary education. Besides, I was not even sure of what I would study if I were to go to university. Rather than stay at home for a year, I opted for nursing.

At Pretoria station I boarded a train to Nelspruit, arriving at four in the morning. I then took a taxi first to White River, and then to Bush, as Bushbuckridge is fondly known. I had no idea where I was heading, either literally or figuratively. Here I was, a Mokgatla girl who had spent her childhood in places like Kgwadubeng, Mosetlha, Mabopane and Mafikeng, suddenly finding myself in a chapel in one of the hottest places in the country, wearing pantyhose and lace-up shoes, a white starched apron and a cap, singing *"Tinsimu"* at a Swiss mission station.

I had never owned, let alone worn, pantyhose in my life, and in the heat I found them unbearable. I have to admit, though, as far as singing *"Tinsimu"* was concerned, *Mfundisi* Ngobe and *Tatana* Makama, Timba, Sowane and Sambo made learning Shangaan very easy. They were all chatty, they greeted and conversed with everyone in Shangaan in the chapel and hospital corridors, and it did not take very long for me to learn the language.

Language is a very powerful transmitter of cultural knowledge and wisdom. If only we could learn to speak as many African languages as possible and learn about other people's cultural practices instead of being buried in a grave of tribalism. If we could do that, reclaiming our heritage as Africans would be much easier and simpler.

In addition to Shangaan, I love Tshivenda. I find the language to be a fascinating combination of many others such as Sesotho, Shangaan, and Shona. Listening to Venda people speak, I recognise myself in the language. I also feel a link with the history of the Guardians of sacred knowledge, our shaman warriors. Invariably, this leads me to contemplate the great kingdoms, the dynasty of Monomotapa, and tales of Great Zimbabwe and the Matombo Hills, as well as many other shrines that were destroyed by missionaries in an attempt to cut Africans off from their prayers.

Many, many years ago when they came to our land, the missionaries found us praying with nature – in caves, on mountaintops, beside rivers and lakes. When they found us talking to the Sun, the Moon and the Stars, they called us uncivilised. When they saw us kneel down in prayer, talking to a plant, *legwama*, they called us primitive. When we gave offerings to the gods, they claimed we worshipped the devil. When they saw us dance in a circle talking to the wind asking for rain, they called us crazy. Because they did not understand our prayers, they condemned us and destroyed our shrines. In time, they made us go to their schools. We changed our names. We learnt their prayers and almost forgot our ancestors. Our languages have suffered as a result.

I persevered in my first year of nursing despite those detestable white caps. I looked on in wonder as some of

130

my colleagues took extra time starching their caps, and even making frills that stuck out at the top. Mine was an unattractive white round object, which I pinned to my head whenever I reported on duty. If I sat on it accidentally, I straightened it out as best I could and just pinned it back on. I simply couldn't see what all the fuss was about, let alone what the role of the cap was.

I received my training from Sister Maylu Malapane, Sister Botteron and others. In the wards, I worked with Drs Golele and Gulube, as well as Dr Robert from Switzerland, who once cheerfully used a stethoscope to examine the head of a patient complaining of a headache. Who can blame him? We believe so much in Western medicine that even an injection of sterile water sends us home satisfied that *o mphile lemao*, yet we are quick to question the effect of *serokolo* from a local healer.

After writing my first-year examinations, I wrote to my parents saying that nursing was definitely not for me. The letter was no sooner sent than I received my results and discovered that I had received top marks. My parents persuaded me to persevere a little longer. Looking back, there were things I hated about nursing, especially its rigid training and practice that seemed to resemble the military. However, I also received a great deal of satisfaction from interacting with all kinds of people who came to hospital, and I have been nurtured by the experience of healing the sick. It was probably the very beginning of my journey as a healer.

My memories of life as a student nurse in Bushbuckridge include interactions with men from Johannesburg, *magoduka* who walked up and down the hospital corridors using interesting pick-up lines in their attempts to chat up the nurses. These men from Joni (which is short for Johannesburg, and includes towns such as Witbank and Brits) all wore colourful pants and shirts, capping the look with a Stetson hat decorated with feathers. Whenever they met a nurse they fancied along the corridor, they proposed marriage. The words "love" or "relationship" never seemed to come up, although "I want to marry you and take you to my mother" was a popular form of persuasion. The very thought of being dumped with someone's snuff-sniffing mother in a remote village, a baby on the way and surrounded by a group of barefoot children while their father went back to his other lover in Joni made some of us run like hares.

I lived in Bushbuckridge for three and a half years, at the end of which I was awarded an integrated diploma in general nursing and midwifery. I am proud to say that I have helped deliver more than 100 babies. At the same time, though, I am most alarmed at how modern society has conditioned women to view childbirth as a costly medical condition. Reliance on medical experts who, unlike midwives, rely on machines for help is only one instance of the overemphasis on technology as opposed to nature's ways. Currently, normal deliveries at home or in state facilities are rapidly being outnumbered by Caesarian sections in private clinics. A natural process previously in the hands of midwives (both traditional and Western) has now been largely transferred to the hands of men trained to rely on specialist interventions.

My mother, who was a midwife in a rural village, tells that there were times when she had to deal with complications, and because there were no ambulances or hospitals nearby, babies' lives were at risk. In spite of these difficulties, my mother believes that those early midwives were the best, effortlessly delivering babies at night in rural clinics with no electricity. I am not in any way denying the reality of the increasing prevalence of maternal deaths and birth complications, especially in rural clinics and hospitals. Yet many of these deaths are the result of poverty, poor nutrition, overwork and lack of support rather than a lack of sophisticated medical intervention. This means that instead of addressing the problem exclusively through high-tech medicine and by hoping to attract more specialists to the rural areas, something that is very unlikely considering the current dilemma with medical aids, we should rather explore other natural, simpler and more cost-effective ways of saving lives.

One of these would be to develop health policies and practices that acknowledge the existence and skills of traditional midwives. Traditional midwifery is part of an ancient reproductive health system, and traditional midwives have played a significant role in health care delivery in supporting women who gave birth at home rather than in hospital. The traditional midwife is given different names in different languages. In Setswana, she is referred to as *mmabotsetse* or *mmelegisi*. In Shona she is referred to as *ambuya*, meaning "grandmother", since in Africa, the traditional midwife is the equivalent of a grandmother. Traditional midwives live in the area in which they practise; they speak the local language and understand local cultural beliefs and practices. Many have learnt their art from working with women experts in their own families or from serving as apprentices to local traditional midwives. A home delivery under the supervision of the traditional midwife offers a mother holistic care that is sensitive to cultural beliefs and practices known to be beneficial to the well-being of the mother and her baby.

To be strictly objective, not all traditional practices are beneficial to the mother's well-being. A few actually limit her choices regarding movement, intimate relationships and nutrition. For instance, according to the traditional system, a pregnant woman is not allowed to eat eggs or liver, which modern health care has shown to be a source of protein and iron respectively. Nevertheless, there are many other traditional beliefs and practices that are known to benefit the mother and the baby.

During labour, a woman who is giving birth is supported and supervised by a woman elder whose role it is to mother the mother – a practice that has been proved in a range of contexts to reduce the need for Caesarian sections significantly. During the traditional birthing process the mother assumes a squatting position over *mmutele*, crushed dried cow dung meant to absorb the blood on the floor. Scientific research has revealed that giving birth while lying down creates excessive pressure, and limits the diameter of the pelvic outlet. Squatting, on the other hand, keeps the pregnant uterus off the major pelvic blood vessels leading to the heart, and so the blood supply from the mother to the baby is improved.

In a traditional setting, the umbilical cord is not cut until the placenta has been delivered. The placenta is buried under a tree in the yard. The act of burying the placenta in a specific place is closely tied to one's spiritual roots. Wars, oppression and the physical displacement of populations have today resulted in spiritual displacement from the places of our biological birth, places where our placenta would have been buried.

After the delivery, a woman is assigned a permanent helper, and a stick is placed at the door of her hut to announce the baby's birth and to limit entry until the stump of the umbilical cord has fallen off. During this time, a woman is given plenty of fluids (water, milk and tea) and foods known to improve healing and milk production. Bottle-feeding never enters the equation: breastfeeding is the only and best option for the baby.

In many ways, this is also a time for the mother to bond with her baby without having to bother about many other household chores (including washing the nappies), as these become the responsibility of other women in the family. Essentially, she is encouraged to rest and enjoy food that she has not had to prepare. Part of this recovery includes taking special herbal preparations meant to strengthen her blood. She is also massaged to alleviate symptoms such as backache. The baby sleeps closer to her and is strengthened with herbs and special spiritual ceremonies. In addition to enhancing the bonding between the mother and the baby, these traditional practices go a long way towards preventing some modern complications such as cot death and post-natal depression.

As a mother of three and a trained midwife, I have experienced childbirth in many different ways. As a Western-trained midwife, I have helped women to deliver their babies lying on a hospital bed. I have also assisted doctors as they performed Caesarian sections in sterile operating theatres. When I fell pregnant with my first child, I received antenatal care at a local clinic with a midwife in attendance and delivered in hospital. My aunt, *Mme* Morongwa, was driven over 300 kilometres from Hammanskraal to Mafikeng and back to perform a special ritual on the baby and to wash soiled nappies.

Because he was the first grandchild of the family, my son was spoiled with love from the whole family. He had

135

colic and would start yelling at around six in the evening until late at night. All my family members, my brothers, sister, father and mother took turns in helping me pacify this little scrap of humanity who seemed determined to deafen us all. At night, as I lay with him in my room, the slightest whimper would summon my father. First he would pick up the baby and take him to his and my mother's bedroom. Then he would be back for the nappy and a bottle of Vaseline. The last trip would be for a blanket to wrap up his little treasure as he snuggled between his grandparents.

During my second pregnancy I was living in Johannesburg, and decided to give technology the benefit of the doubt. I started antenatal care with a specialist, but stopped making appointments when I realised how expensive it was to have my blood pressure checked and my urine tested, and instead went to a hospital-based facility run by midwives. I delivered my daughter on a cold and cloudy Saturday afternoon in hospital. In a day or so, we went home. She was much quieter and more peaceful than my first baby, and did nothing but feed and sleep. Ironically, as she grows into a young woman, she is now louder than her big brother.

My third pregnancy was completely different. I was much older and wiser and was spending a considerable amount of time with women elders in the villages. At that point in my life, I was also approaching a peaceful place as far as accepting my role as being a healer was concerned. I was in my late thirties, and from the onset I worked with a midwife who lived a few houses away, preparing for a home birth. Apart from the actual delivery, which happened at a local clinic to avoid possible complications, the whole process took place at home. When the membranes ruptured, the midwife noticed that the waters were stained with meconium – a sign of foetal distress. Preferring to be cautious, she drove us to a nearby clinic, where she helped to deliver the baby in no time. Afterwards, the baby was checked and wrapped up and the midwife drove us straight back home.

In all of my pregnancies, I have combined Western medicine with traditional health care. I know the sensation of having my back massaged by the firm and loving hands of a woman elder whose main mission is to love my body back to health. I know what it feels like to breast-feed my baby after having enjoyed a meal prepared by my mother. I have, throughout my entire reproductive life, participated in traditional ceremonies and rituals led by healers and elders in my family. There is no need for Africa to be ashamed of its own healers and only to consult them away from prying eyes in the dark of the night. For me, visiting a healer is no different from visiting a specialist in a modern consulting room. While the Western and traditional health systems each have a unique role to play in my life, however, I find myself using Western medicine less and less.

Needless to say, because I have the means to prevent disease, I can afford the choices I make in health care. In contrast, many women in my country hardly have the means to ward off preventable illness. Their day-to-day existence is a struggle to survive against the odds, to fill up empty stomachs. Our choice of health care therefore depends very much on our state of economic and spiritual well-being. Poverty alleviation measures and respect for people's cultural and spiritual beliefs should play a central role in the maternal and child health policies of any country.

I left Masana Hospital to work as a registered nurse in the casualty department of Ga Rankuwa Hospital for two years before leaving to study for a degree at the University of the North, where I majored in Psychology, Nursing Education and Community Health. I spent my time at Ga Rankuwa suturing lacerations on the bodies of a great number of men, mostly from Ramogodi, Winterveldt and Oukasie. It was also at this time that I encountered a number of women who had been severely injured after being attacked by men in their lives. It was in this experience that my work in the area of violence against women began to take root. At the time I did know what to do about the situation except to suture the lacerations and give medication. Silently, though, I prayed that one day I would find ways of addressing this serious crime against women that would go beyond a limited medical model of intervention.

Questioning a limited and oppressive model of nursing training was later to be the focus of research that I undertook with a colleague at the Centre for the Study of Health Policy at Wits Medical School. When I presented the findings at a seminar in Pretoria in 1989 I was almost eaten alive by one Professor Grobelaar from Unisa for commenting that nursing education produced subservient and stereotyped individuals who never questioned orders from above. However, at that time many nurses viewed health care as something separate from politics, since politics involved fighting for power and against inequality, actions in which they had been led to believe they had no role to play. These views were even more strongly held by black nurses, who had received an inferior education and had been socialised to believe in their inferiority.

Because nursing is a career that has always been easily accessible to women, it has the potential to be used as a liberating tool. Freedom from oppression, however, required a rejection of the stereotypical and oppressive nature of nursing education. From the study that my colleague and I conducted, it was clear that while most of the nurses interviewed had some understanding of the effects of political and socio-economic factors on health, their understanding was superficial and did not influence their attitude, actions and behaviour. Instead, many of the nurses blamed communities for their ignorance rather than recognising that deeply entrenched political factors were contributing to ill health. Although many were aware of the injustices in health care, they were afraid to speak out for fear of victimisation by nursing authorities and because of the way they had been socialised as women. Many nurses are concerned about professionalism. Certainly this is valid, but what is also required is an acknowledgement of the challenges that nurses are facing, including racism in nursing, so that they can provide leadership in the present health care crisis.

A review of history in South Africa must include a review of nursing history that acknowledges more than just the role of white nurses who were, by virtue of their easy access to quality education, well positioned to introduce changes within the field. While many of these interventions benefited the profession positively, others were racist and hampered the development of black nurses. Even though racism in nursing is a reality, it is rarely addressed openly and honestly. Black nurses are in the majority and form the backbone of health care delivery in rural South Africa in particular. Their working conditions should therefore reflect a conscious recognition that they are not just pairs of black hands, but compatriots committed to quality of life for all. Without them, our health services are doomed to collapse, and this may soon become a reality given the exodus to countries such as Saudi Arabia, Britain and the United States.

Having left Bushbuckridge many years ago, I recently visited what is now Mapulaneng Hospital on my way back from Acornhoek. The hospital surroundings were clean and certainly very different from some of the urban hospitals that have become so filthy that you would not consider them a place for health and healing. Everything looked the same except for the large number of undertakers.

The reality is, we are sinking as a nation. HIV/Aids, violence and other preventable diseases of poverty continue inexorably to claim the lives of both young and old. Faced with the increasing prevalence of HIV/Aids in Africa, we are challenged to develop a scientific awareness and treatment campaign that is rooted in ancient teachings that focus on healing beyond the physical. Unlike the current exclusive focus on scientific research and Western interventions, such a campaign will acknowledge the powerful role that African values play in the prevention of any illness. Modern scientific interventions need to be adapted to draw on some of the most fundamental teachings inherent in African healing systems.

This kind of multidisciplinary intervention will be in line with the current call for an African Renaissance aimed at uplifting African civilisation. The union of science, spirit and community-building, the combination of drugs with herbs, prayers and rituals will go a long way towards restoring a balance to people's healing systems. While the billions of dollars in foreign aid for Aids is welcome, Africa must match it with an equal amount of determination and reclamation of ancient wisdom as a means of healing.

Aid for Aids is about accomplishing
an impossible dream
not because we are wealthy or wise
but because it's time to face our ruins
beneath the shadow of death
with our wounds gaping, our soul wailing
faces twisted, screams muffled
yet
aided by the light of ancestral fire
travelling to a place of our becoming.
No wealthy man or powerful government
stands to make a profit from such a mission
because the soul of my ancestors
unlike their land and children
is not for sale.

As I drove back home from Mapulaneng through Marite, I was reminded of all the men we treated for very serious injuries, most of whom came from this area. What is it about Marite that makes it so violent? I noticed any number of restaurant and eating house signs in shops that do not sell much to eat, but enough to drink. I also noticed how many billboards advertised alcohol.

Liquor companies need to be held accountable for a degree of the dis-eased mental state of the majority of men in poor black communities. Go to any village, township or informal settlement across the country and count the number of taverns and liquor stores compared with other development and business ventures. This is a job creation strategy, some may argue. But it is also a self-annihilation strategy. The impact of alcohol on our families and communities is well known. So many black artists, intellectuals, leaders and visionaries have crumbled under the might of this disease. We are a nation that does not know how to heal our wound. Instead, we search for ways of numbing the pain.

We have to admit that we are victims of various forms of addictive thoughts, patterns and behaviour, a situation which is further compounded by our vulnerability to the power of irresponsible advertising on radio, television and in the print media. It is time to name our pain.

Health is not just the absence of physical illness, but the presence of a positive psychological and spiritual sense of self. Unless we confront racism, sexism and poverty, we as South Africans will never achieve cultural equity and true health.

Learning to love without fear

I have spent time going through some of my earlier journal entries. In some ways, I feel as if I haven't moved much. In other ways, though, I have made significant progress. I have worked damn hard on myself. For a long time I was reluctant to face what I myself had done to contribute to my own unhappiness and pain. It is always easier to blame others for one's failures rather than interrogating oneself, asking: Am I in any way contributing to my unhappiness? If so, what can I do to change the situation? What do I stand to gain from staying stuck in an unhappy situation? If there is no benefit, no trade-off, why am I still here?

After all the hard work, I have arrived at a point where I am becoming comfortable with looking at my image in the mirror, facing my shadow side. One of the most fundamental steps in the journey to healing is to acknowledge and accept our shadow, that part of ourselves that we dislike and have even repressed or rejected. In an era that encourages values such as success, competitiveness, courage, resilience and power, there is often no room left to express feelings of vulnerability, fear and failure. While it is important to express positive energies, it is equally important not to disown the negative aspects lest they go underground and from there continue to rule our life's choices.

It has taken me several years to grasp this important lesson. Pride, arrogance and the false belief that I was one of the best things to have arrived on planet Earth conveniently covered my shadow. Such an attitude is not healthy for any relationship with the self and with others. Many of us believe that anyone lucky enough to be in a relationship with us must work damn hard to keep it that way. This essentially means that our lovers must dance to our music. We become controlling because we feel insecure.

Whether we suffer from an inferiority or a superiority complex, it is an indication of an internal imbalance often rooted in fear and insecurity. If you are secure, there is no way that you will set out to control others. If you accept yourself fully, you will have no difficulty in accepting others, including those with different views and beliefs. As *Tata* Rolihlahla Mandela tells us: "A man who takes away another man's freedom is a prisoner of hatred, he is locked behind the bars of prejudice and narrow-mindedness. I am not truly free if I am taking away someone else's freedom, just as surely as I am not free when my freedom is taken from me".[11]

Freedom. So many women and men all over the world have lived and died for freedom, for national liberation. But while nations have fought for their liberation, how many of us have been willing to seek the highest form of liberation, freedom to be true to the self? How many of us are willing to confront our dark sides and let the light banish the shadow? How many of us have the courage to live our lives fully and consciously in spite of the fear?

It has been during the toughest times in my life that I have found strength in women's writing and poetry from across the world, such as this poem by Anna Akhmatova[12], which spoke to me of true wealth in the days when I suffered bitter material hardship:

[11] Mandela, N.R. 1994. *Long Walk to Freedom: The Autobiography of Nelson Mandela*. South Africa: Macdonald Purnell: p.617.
[12] Akhmatova, A. 1989. *Selected Poems*. UK: Harvill Press.

If all who have begged help
From me in this world,
All the holy innocents,
Broken wives, and cripples,
The imprisoned, the suicidal –
If they had sent me one kopeck
I should have become 'richer
Than all Egypt'...
But they did not send me kopecks,
Instead they shared with me their strength,
And so nothing in the world
Is stronger than I,
And I can bear anything, even this.

As I think back on my life, I see that I have done well in many spheres of my life; I have survived the odds. However, I have continued to be ruled by fear in relationships. It took me some time to see the light, and in the process, there have been people who have borne the brunt of my insecurity. I forgive myself and ask for forgiveness for having hurt others because of being imprisoned by my own fear.

I am grateful to have been given an opportunity to renew my existence on this earth. Years ago, after surviving a physically violent relationship, I became a spokesperson for women abused by men. Now, I look back and acknowledge that I have looked down on men, ridiculed them and used words to attack them. Admitting to my shadow does not in any way mean that I deserved the violence. But I must accept and embrace my dark side, although this is difficult and painful, because if I don't, I will never open up to my healing.

When a woman leaves an abusive relationship, she

takes her mind with her. While her abuser may be absent physically, the abused woman may nevertheless continue to be ruled by fear and an ongoing need to avenge her trauma. Leaving an abusive relationship is not the end but the beginning of a painful healing process.

While many abused women have courageously moved away from a physically violent space, some continue to live their lives driven and ruled by their abusive thought patterns. I chose to leave. I also took my wounds with me and it was some time before I could accept that even though I had left, I was still being abused – not by someone else, but by myself, because I had become an expert at self-abuse and self-sabotage. Moving from one unhealthy relationship to another, I finally had to stop and ask: What is happiness and where can I get it? The answer came from deep inside: "You are the source of your happiness. Happiness is a choice you make in spite of who is in your life or what is going on in your life". It was only when I took full responsibility for my own healing and liberation as a woman that I understood why it was futile to expect someone else to make me happy while I failed to secure my own happiness.

Some women choose to stay and work on the relationship from within by changing the Self and the Other. While changing the Other may not be entirely out of the question, the growth of the Self should always remain paramount. If you are involved in an abusive relationship and you do not really believe in your own goodness, but seek counselling only for the purpose of changing the other's violent behaviour, chances are you will miss out on profound moments of personal growth. Besides, if the violence does not stop, you might feel that counselling has failed. However, you have to realise that men's violence is their problem and they will have to face it honestly without resorting to excuses such as "she provoked me" or "this is a man's world and she is my woman".

There is no excuse for violence. Yet a violent person will make anything and everything a reason: noisy children, a meal not served on time, losing a job. To minimise their guilt, abusers transfer the responsibility for their violent acts to their victims, accusing them of provoking the abuse. Certainly, there is not much we can do about how people act towards us, as we have no control over what they choose to do to us. What we do have full control over, though, is how we react and respond to them. Our responses and reactions to situations and people are our choices. "I hit her because she made me mad" simply does not hold. The violence belongs to the abuser. He chooses to express his anger violently. His healing should therefore not depend on the woman's stopping a behaviour that provokes him, but on his wanting to change for the better through exploring other ways of expressing anger.

Our healing, therefore, is a personal choice dependent not on external factors, but on our determination and courage to seek help from within. This approach to healing is difficult and unpopular because it does not allow us to wallow in blame and self-pity. Instead, it calls us to take charge of our own healing. By saying this, I am by no means ignoring the fact that violence against women is founded on the false belief that women are men's property. For that to change, we need to dismantle the socio-economic and political apparatus that is biased against women. Similarly, by advocating for personal healing and liberation I do not disregard the fact that the wounds suffered by the majority of South Africans are the result of a gross legacy of economic deprivation and political repression that has slashed and cut away at people's sense of self. Personal healing and liberation need to be supported by external corrective measures such as poverty alleviation, improvement in the criminal justice system as well as access to resources such as education.

By citing poverty alleviation as a counter measure, I don't mean to imply that violence affects poor black families only. We know from reports and experience that family violence knows no colour, creed or class. Nor do I mean to imply that the poor who have no formal education lack the intellectual or spiritual means to address the problem. Ancient interventions, while not recorded in textbooks, are many and varied.

Taking charge of our healing remains the most painful, most difficult but most definite way to every woman and man's inner peace. As we set out on this path, we will practise being gentle with ourselves, and therefore hurt ourselves less. As we learn to hurt ourselves less, we will know and believe that we are loving and lovable and that we do not deserve abuse from anyone. As we learn to practise self-love, we will also know and believe that everyone is loving and lovable and that no one deserves to be subjected to our violence. If we hit out at others (in word or deed) and they in turn stand up to us, we will know that they are acting within their rights as well as from a position of self-love.

Having had the time to reflect on my life as well as the lives of the many women and men whom I have encountered in my work, I am committed to creating healing circles for women and men. I was introduced to this concept during my visit to a shelter for abused women of indigenous communities in Canada in 1996. I learnt from my hosts that elders in the community followed a powerful strategy to end violence against women. Instead of using crisis-oriented strategies that punish the abuser by separating him from family, the elders had introduced a concept of healing that recognises the effect of violence on both the victim and the offender, as well as their families and the community. This concept is founded on a search for harmony, healing and balance within the entire system. This holistic view is derived from the medicine wheel. The wheel represents the harmonious interconnectedness of the physical, the mental, the emotional and the spiritual. The overall balance determines the overall health and well-being of an individual. The medicine wheel teaches that spirituality is the purest form of political conscience.

It is from embarking on my own spiritual path and from contact with elders that I welcome with deep gratitude the opportunity to learn to love without anger and fear. I always knew that I had power, but I did not really know how to be powerful. All human beings are powerful, yet very few know how to relate to it. We are all inherently loving and caring, yet few know how to love without being controlling. Love is not about control; it is not about making decisions and choices for others. Learning not to control is founded on loving without conditions and the ability to let go, to let things be.

This lesson was brought home to me one afternoon as I lay under a tree in my garden. I noticed a little ant trapped in a dish. In its attempt to get back to the grass, it flipped over several times. Every time it fell, I watched with amazement how it used all its power and strength to get back on track. After it had fallen for the fourth time, I intervened, and tilted the dish. But as I did so, the spoon that had been resting in the dish slid forward and crushed the ant. That was the ultimate lesson in just letting things be. I ought not to have intervened – the ant could have made it on its own. It was not my job to tilt the dish; ultimately the ant would have found its way back to the grass. I realised that often our inability to let go results in unintended damage. Our obsession to rescue others may also be an attempt to exercise some form of control. This is an indication of our inner imbalance, and it is not good for us or for the people we are rescuing. By casting ourselves as rescuer and substitute for their Creator, we interfere with their connection to their source of light. This is a very important lesson. All human beings have an innate capacity to grow and triumph over hardships and life's challenges. We need to acknowledge our weaknesses with a view to entering into a reconstructive dialogue with those hidden parts that continue to rule our lives. Once we allow ourselves to meet our self-deceptions, fears and lies head-on, the process of healing will begin.

One of the greatest fears to overcome is the fear of being alone. If you are reading this book and you are alone in your cute pad with your stylish car parked downstairs and your cell phone silent because suddenly you seem not to be popular anymore, don't despair. If you are one of the privileged minority who owns CDs, pick out the music that you love best, run a hot bath, dim the lights. Light candles, incense or anything that will engage your senses and warm your spirit. Take time in the bath, meditate if you can. Give yourself permission to feel. There may not be another person there, but you are not alone. You are in good company, spending an exclusive reflective evening with one of the greatest human beings ever created on this planet – you. Take a moment to thank your Creator for your existence. Note that you have the luxury of a hot bath while many others do not have a drop to drink. Without any guilt feelings, ask to be guided to live your life in a way that gives to others. There are many ways of giving, but the best is to live your life fully and well.

Living your life fully and well means many things, such as letting go of the urge to make a grand appearance at a hot party or a social event as a way of filling up an inner void. Parties can be a soul killer, if we let them. Being addicted to company that makes us question and doubt who we are is not good for our health. We are more and better than what we are made to believe, and the beautiful thing is we don't have to prove our magnificence to anyone.

Living your life fully may also include switching off your cell phone when you go to bed, releasing yourself from the hope that after being out with the boys or girls in the early hours of the morning, he'll dial your number. An empty, purely physical relationship is nothing but a one-way ticket straight to hell. That kind of life is artificial. It's just a fake, worth nothing. We cannot continue to think so little of ourselves. How ironic that we women complain that men don't take our liberation seriously, yet we don't believe in our own worth or our right to a special existence on earth. Loving in constant fear of being dumped, we behave in outrageous ways that make us cringe with shame once we are alone with our conscience.

One of the greatest favours that we can all do for ourselves is to overcome the fear of being dumped by a lover. I'll be the first to admit that releasing an attachment to someone is excruciatingly painful, but it's essential. How can we give and receive love when we are trapped in fear? How can we live our truth if we remain imprisoned by the need to be in a relationship, any relationship, by any means necessary? Susan Jeffers puts it so well when she says "[w]e look for wholeness through our mates; hence, not only are we afraid of being abandoned, but we are also afraid to leave. Our fear of abandonment creates our need to possess and control. Our fear of leaving creates our need to create the 'perfect' man so that we won't have to leave".[13]

It is crucial for us to stand tall in loving kindness, on our own. It is equally important that we envision the men in our lives standing strongly in love on their own. The common notion of men not being able to live without us is nothing but an excuse to tend our fragile ego. Men can make it on their own, and so can we. We are a special gift to the world, and so are men.

[13] Jeffers, S. 1996. *Opening Our Hearts to Men*. London: Piatkus: p.186.

Soular eclipse

Where does the Moon disappear to when we cannot see her in the sky? Where is she tonight, two days before the solar eclipse? Could she be preparing for her meeting with the Sun? He gives light during the day; she gives light at night. Where is the Moon tonight, when I need her most?

Although I am driving along a familiar road to the mountainous north, I have never driven this route at night. I cannot see the mountains in the dark; I can only feel them. These stars are forever. They have been here before and they will be here in the future. Looking above, I notice that those stars that shine only dimly tend to gather together to form a village. Do they perhaps feel the need to share their light? I also notice that those that shine brightest appear self-assured and stand out from the rest. I remember what the great prophet, *Mme* Morongwa, says about the stars – that we each have a special star assigned to us, and that each star in the universe represents a sacred gift. Just as some of the stars are hidden from our eyes, some of our talents lie deep, and it is only when we search profoundly that we find the light.

When I see stars, I also think of *Mme* Makhubedu, our very own Professor of Astronomy. She has never set foot in a university or a planetarium; she has never looked through a telescope, yet she knows so much about the moon and the stars. Our astronomers don't have a piece of paper as evidence of their knowledge and wisdom. For centuries, they have lived on earth with the star-studded sky serving as both an electric blanket and a computer screen at night. They have lived and communicated with the moon and the stars. They carry their knowledge and wisdom in them. It is a part of who they are and it comes from Africa. As our beloved father and poet, Don Mattera, keeps reminding us, we have been here before, with diamonds glittering at our feet. We have been here before.

As I drive through this area, with its familiar bends, hills and valleys, the only other vehicles are the big trucks. Where are they going and what are they transporting? Who are the owners of these trucks, and where are they at this hour of the night? Are they related to the Du Toits, the Van der Merwes, the Bothas? Are they in their homes with their families? Visiting friends and family, perhaps, having a *braai*, a family get-together, or planning a *mampoerfees* for the coming weekend? It is at such community events that families gather together to enjoy food, drink, music and human connection, and celebrate life. Whatever happened to our own rituals and gatherings?

Who are the men behind the steering wheels of the trucks? Are they descendants of the Ndous, the Makhubelas, the Mashigos? Where do they come from, and where are their families at this hour of the night? What kind of a meal, if any, did their children have this evening? Do their children have access to any education, or do they work on the same farm as their parents? Some of the drivers will have left their families in remote villages – when last did they get home to be with their wives and children? Where are they going to sleep tonight, and with whom?

I cannot help thinking of the multitude of black men living on the road and sleeping with strange partners at various truck stops. How many of them have contracted the HI virus? During their infrequent visits home, can their wives ever have the courage to refuse sex without a condom? How many married and monogamous women will be infected? How many children will be born with the virus? How many Aids orphans will the country have?

My vision blurred with tears at this thought, I call on the healers residing in the mountain to help my country to love and care for itself. I appeal to *Bo-Rakgolo ba metsi* residing in the depths of Lepelle to reach out to us and give us the courage to heal. Our ship is sinking and we do not really know who we are and where we are going. We live the superficial and soul-less way of life that we have accepted from the hands of the capitalists and cultural imperialists. I remember the painful lament of Langston Hughes, that we are quick to defer our dreams, we watch them dry up like a raisin in the sun. Our dreams represent our essence. If they dry up, we are dead.

And it is on this night that I connect for the very first time with the spirit of my sister, whom I never knew. My parents once told me that I had another sister, Bontle, who was born after me but died in infancy. Connecting with her spirit for the first time is the most beautiful experience. She does not give me any specific message, but places a wonderful smile in my heart.

How do I explain my first meeting with my sister a mere 48 hours before the first solar eclipse of the new century? It is not anything I can explain. All I can do is thank her. Thank you, my dear sister, for the reunion; please look out for me and our sister Lenyalo, who is very tender and special – *ke ngwana wa ngwako.*

As the Moon meets the Sun at their special pre-arranged rendezvous in Africa on 21 June 2001, may it be a moment of return to our roots. It is no coincidence that the first total eclipse of the new millennium should be witnessed in Zambia, a place where a great number of exiled South Africans spent the greater part of their lives as combatants fighting a racist minority regime.

Seven years into the new political era, we pray for the wit, courage and persistence to participate in the much-needed spiritual revolution. It is through the fusion of the political and spiritual revolution that we can turn our houses into homes. As Rachelle Ferrell puts it in her song, "Peace on earth":

How can we heal the wounds of the world
If we cannot heal our own?
And where does this peace on earth begin
If not in the home?[14]

May the calls for peace, love and abundance in Africa translate into a peaceful and loving co-existence in our hearts and our homes. May the Goddess bless Africa and her children.

[14] Rachelle Ferrell. 1992. Rachelle Ferrell. Capital Records Inc.

Alone in company,
accompanied in solitude

By nature, I am domesticated. Unbound and carefree, but domesticated. I am inspired by the bird that flies high above the mountains, away from its nest in solitude, only to come back to its home later. We all need a home. While mention of a home brings to mind the image of a physical space, I think that what we yearn for most is a spiritual home; a place where we are accepted unconditionally just the way that we are. It is from this place that we can venture out to engage with the world, irrespective of whether it is accepting of us or not.

I find it such a pity that government housing policies tend to focus only on providing a physical shelter. At one level, so many people live in the streets without a roof over their head. Yet at another level, millions have a roof over their head and gaping holes in their heart. While government makes some effort to address the problem of physical homelessness, very little attention is given to spiritual homelessness. As a nation, we continue to be alienated from the self, at both individual and collective level.

I have never been without a physical home. I am one of the privileged few, and for that I am deeply grateful. I have been spiritually homeless at various points in my life, however. I know the feeling of being in a comfortable home that I have worked hard for, yet not having a sense of being at home. I have experienced emptiness and a void in my soul, which made me crave external recognition and approval. I know what it is like to be alienated from the self to the point where you don't even recognise who and where you are, or how you got there in the first place. I have felt the pangs of loneliness and looked solitude in the eye many times. I know what it is like to be with someone yet feel lonely, to feel alone while in company. And for all this I am grateful. How else would I have learnt to appreciate the feeling of being accompanied in solitude? How else would I have been compelled to search for an inner compass, to find a way back home?

It is from the comfort of a spiritual home that I am able to reflect and learn from my life experiences in this lifetime, and from other people. It is from this space that, when I read through the society pages of some of our local newspapers and magazines, I wonder about our interpretation of the notion of the human being as a social animal. I cannot help but notice that for some, a social life has ceased to be fun, and has been reduced to the relentless task of keeping their name on the A list. Could it be a case of papering over the spiritual cracks? A manifestation of a deep longing for a sense of belonging? From my vantage point, all the parading, the pretence and the posing seem like hard work. No wonder these events are called functions. They are hard work, hard play.

That sets me thinking about the role of play and fun in our lives. I have had the privilege of partying with all kinds of people in a variety of surroundings. I remember having the times of my life in Alexandra. In a feel-good mood driving home from Alex after a night of dancing, dancing and more dancing, I would send some positive energy to those of my contemporaries who asked worriedly, "But is it safe in Alex?" I have also played with white South Africans in some of the suburbs of Johannesburg, all the while fighting the choking feeling of being like a foreigner in my own country. As a heterosexual black woman, I have also given myself permission to indulge in wild parties with gay white friends both in South Africa and abroad.

Undoubtedly, and naturally, there was a time in my life when I would not have felt comfortable playing on such a variety of playgrounds. I do not in any way mean to suggest that I am now capable of occupying all and any kind of space. What I am saying is that I have, in both work and play, had ample opportunity to redefine and sometimes even dismantle a significant number of psychological walls behind which so many of us continue to hide. Can you imagine what this world would be like if we could all find the strength, courage and wit to demolish our own private Berlin Walls? Would we still need billions of dollars to host international conferences on racism, sexism, homophobia, or any other kind of discrimination?

It took time, energy and determination to erect those walls. Unfortunately, the process of taking them down requires the very same ingredients. Some walls come down almost without our being aware of it, yet others require constant vigilance lest they spring up again the moment our backs are turned.

Like all black people, I have suffered dislocations resulting from repeated psychological blows, and I have been consumed by intense rage and hatred in many of my encounters with white people. There is, however, a limit to what I can take as a person. Other people who are different from me may choose to oppress me from the outside, but I refuse to oppress myself from the inside. They may look at me and see a woman or a black person and nothing more. That is their limited view. I am much deeper, brighter and bigger than meets the physical eye. I am whole; who I am is enough, I am complete.

For those of us who dare to search for unconventional ways of becoming, the issue of racism is not limited to a theoretical critique of the status quo. It is also about inner consciousness work, and it includes confronting inner thoughts that present an obstacle to our healing. In her book, *The Bluest Eye*[15], Toni Morrison asserts that many of us turn away from reality because the pain of awareness is unbearable. But it is only by becoming aware, by facing our reality and our suffering, that we see things clearly.

In my endeavour to love and embrace my blackness without rage, I need to face the challenge of accepting that white people can love their whiteness without guilt. In my quest to connect with my femininity, I open my heart to images of men loving their masculinity. As I take what are sometimes faltering steps on the path of wholeness I become conscious and take ownership of my own oppressive thoughts – "What did you expect, she's Jewish"; "*Ke letebele*"; "He's a man". I will take the time I need to reclaim the purity of my yesterday as well as redefine my existence as a *Motswana*, a woman and an African in this lifetime. Healing and forgiveness lie at the core of that redefinition.

[15] Morrison, T. 1970. *The Bluest Eye*. New York: Pocket Books.

Searching for a matriarchal African spirituality

Many feminists have protested at the scarcity of black women leaders globally. Even though the literature abounds with references to male leaders, South Africa is gradually witnessing a change in this regard. More women in general, and more black women in particular, are becoming involved in the active running of the country from within political, business and community-based structures.

This change is taking place against the backdrop of a number of traditional practices that are still disempowering to women. High maternal death rates as well as physical, sexual and emotional abuse further undermine women's capacity to contribute fully to the country's economy and future prosperity. Young and married women have been identified as the groups that are most vulnerable to HIV.

It has been a struggle for women to find a voice beyond their role as mothers. It has been a further struggle for women to redefine women's health as extending beyond maternal and reproductive issues to include other political, economic, and socio-cultural factors that affect their well-being. The many layers of oppression along race, class and gender lines and what is perceived to be women's passive acceptance of these have called the existence of working-class led feminism in Africa into question.

While literature on the struggle against imperialism acknowledges the powerful role played by male workers, a perusal of feminist literature does not reveal the same degree of reference to the role played by working-class women in the struggle for women's emancipation. Instead, rural and working class women are often viewed as beneficiaries of policies and services rather than as leaders and agents of change. Instead of establishing partnerships with working-class women, finding ways of amplifying their voices and facilitating processes that allow them to speak for themselves, feminists, white and black, have assumed the role of spokespersons and speak on their behalf.

In my work with rural women I have witnessed subtle but powerful ways of resistance and independent thinking related to matters of family reconstruction and gender relations. The lives of rural women, rather than being miserable and hopeless, are pregnant with immense strength, wit and courage in confronting oppression in both the public and private sphere. Some of the feminist views I had adopted from foreign practice and literature have been radically challenged in my work with rural women on issues of gender, sexuality, and HIV. In many ways, my eyes and soul have been opened to a wealth of information found in the midst of our kind, our mothers and grandmothers. It is from them that I have learnt that in respecting our partners, we gain respect. I have learnt that submission is not necessarily a sign of weakness, but recognition of one's own innate power as well as the power of the other. The fact that one is powerful does not render others less powerful. Being powerful has nothing to do with being better than others, but has a lot to do with being the best that one can be.

The most powerful individuals I know are humble. One of the many significant lessons I have learnt from rural women is that humility involves seeing oneself in relation to the other, as well as putting oneself in a lesser position in order to understand the other holistically.

It was at a rural workshop on African culture and gender violence that I facilitated in Kgomo Kgomo in 1997 that I learnt about the concept of *go hupa kotana*, which literally means keeping a stick in your mouth to prevent you from talking – the English equivalent would be "don't answer back". When I heard this for the first time, my initial reaction was to reject it outright because it reminded me so much of what girls growing up are told: never answer back when a man speaks to you. To my mind, that reinforced the voicelessness imposed on women the world over. However, when I explored this concept further with women elders, I gained a new insight. Yes, the expression does mean that a woman should not answer back. However, there is more to this silence than simple subservience. The difference, these women elders explained, is that not answering back is a conscious and strategic choice rather than a reaction rooted in fear of the repercussions, which may even include a physical beating. Learning to choose our battles and how we fight them, they explained, is one of the most crucial strategies that anyone requires in the fight against dominant forces.

I have spent time discussing this and other lessons with my colleague, Nteseng, who has now taken over as Director of ADAPT. She told me that her grandmother used to tell her *"Nke le ithute go fenngwa"*, meaning "Allow yourself not to win all your battles" – in other words, there is value in losing too. This, of course, is closely tied to the ability to practise humility. In my view, it is essential for both women and men to revisit this very crucial element in our interaction. The sexes have been so tightly locked in battle for so long that we have forgotten how to interact in the most natural and humane way.

The world is crying out for a leadership that is founded on spiritual values of sharing, compassion, interdependence and mutual respect. In this as in other life matters that involve humanity and human relationships, Africa is well positioned to lead the way. I am grateful to be part of a nation that is embarking on a search for sacred spiritual spaces and reclaiming ancient transformative and liberatory tools used by our elders over decades and centuries.

One such space is the village of Dikebu in the district of Makapanstad, a region led by the late *Kgosi* Seaparankwe Makapan.

On 25 May 1969, *Mme* Kubele Motsei, married into the Motaung family, who was at the time a domestic worker employed by Mrs Levine of 28 African Street, Orchards, Johannesburg, had a revelation. *Mme* Kubele, now called Mother Toloki because she has the power to communicate directly with the ancestors, was in the maid's room when, with her physical eyes, she saw ancestors in her room. For several consecutive days, after cleaning the madam's house and doing all the other menial chores that domestic workers do, she returned to her room to interact with her ancestors.

On 5 August 1969, one of her great-grandfathers came to her to announce the arrival of a very important guest. She was made to kneel down facing the door just before midnight. Instead of opening in the normal way, the door cracked down the middle to let in a blinding light, followed by the appearance of Jesus Christ, now called Rara Konyana. As His spirit in the flesh filled the room, a blue cloth covering utensils on a tray on a table mysteriously caught fire. *Mme* Kubele quickly extinguished the fire with her bare hands, and was left with a burn mark on her right hand. Rara Konyana called her name several times, but because she was frozen with fear, she only managed to respond with a whisper after the third call. Announcing his mission to her, the Lord told her that she had been chosen by the Holy Spirit and that from that day onwards, He would dwell in her so that she would become Him in her.

She was told of the dawning of the Third world, the time of the reclamation of African spirituality, and of the return of the Holy Spirit to Africa to heal and spiritually liberate all people of African descent. In the new century, the world would turn to Africa for guidance. New knowledge and a spiritual curriculum would be developed by the ancestors of all races and religions, *Badimo ba ba kgobokaneng*, and taught in the classes of Sewagodimo Spiritual School. The sick would be nursed back to physical, emotional and spiritual health by the ancient healers of Africa, visible and invisible, as well as by Western healers led by the compassionate healing power of Florence Nightingale, in the sacred rooms of Candle Hospital. In the past, in the time of the Second world, the Holy Spirit came through a white person and a man. In the time of the Third world and in Africa, the Spirits would heal the world and communicate through a black person, and a woman.

Because she was black, a woman, and from the working class, with limited formal education, Mother

Toloki was afraid and reluctant to receive and practise the gift. She thought that white people or those with certificates from leading institutions of the world would be the ones to save the planet. Over time, the ancestors taught her that answering such a special and sacred calling is not dependent on any earthly certificates and credentials. The ancestors supported her and helped her work through her fear, as they could not allow this to stand in the way of what must be. A time of healing for Africa has come. Mother Toloki is the chosen one. A black maid with a rural upbringing and with no earthly qualifications is the One.

Upon receiving her gift, she was asked to go back to her village in Kgomo Kgomo to share the vision with her own people and practise her gift by founding Tshenolo the Holy Church, which now has its headquarters in Dikebu. On leaving her place of formal employment as a domestic worker and ending her economic dependence on white people, Mother Toloki was informed by her ancestors that she would never again work for anyone. Under the spiritual direction of Rara Konyana and the ancestors, she would be the channel through which Africa would receive the means to regain its wealth, health and wisdom.

The church that she founded under the guidance of the Ancestral Voice, Tshenolo, is not simply a church building. It is a sacred space that also accommodates a spiritual health centre called Candle Hospital. At this healing facility, spiritually anointed healers are directed by the Voice to diagnose and treat ailments. Included in this category are traditional midwives who, through the guidance of the Voice, palpate the baby in the uterus and can even tell the sex of the baby as well as the day and time it will be born. Some practitioners are X-ray specialists. Mother Toloki has informed us that the ancestors are not happy with the high rate of surgical operations being performed, because African people have been used as guinea pigs for far too long. As a result, the ancestors will encourage and make possible surgical operations that do not involve cutting the body.

The sacred space that is Tshenolo also houses an educational institution whose teaching is based on African philosophy and theology. During the Sewagodimo Spiritual School sessions, which are held in Dikebu on the first Saturday of the month, lessons are taught by spiritually anointed professors and teachers. The curriculum includes teachings from Thabo University, whose curriculum is drafted under the guidance of the Voice. Graduates of the programme emerge as African writers, poets, composers and philosophers. All along, Africans have believed white people to be more intelligent and better that they are. According to Mother Toloki's teachings, people of European descent are not better off, but merely received the gift of the teachings of the Voice in another era. In this era, the African century, the gift is assigned to Africa.

The church has followers from throughout South Africa. In addition, it receives visitors, including traditional leaders and visionaries, from beyond the Limpopo and across the Atlantic. In Dikebu, Mother Toloki, *dingaka* (spiritual healers) and *barutisi* (teachers and professors, both male and female) care for the sick and teach the new heavenly curriculum. *Baruti* (priests), who are of both sexes, are chosen by the Voice through Mother Toloki. Both women and men are encouraged to serve on local and regional church committees, and in that way to participate in the affairs of the church. Rara Konyana and the ancestors, through Mother Toloki, have the final say in church affairs.

The congregation consists of women, men and young people called *bakwadi*, or graduates. The graduates are inspired by the ancestors to write poetry, music and messages for fellow members using local languages, idioms and common sayings that people understand and relate to.

Members of the church celebrate Christmas in May instead of December, because Mother Toloki received the gift in the month of May. As part of the celebration at this time, members of the church showcase their colourful and traditional dress, drama, dance, song, and praise poetry. Young women and men dance to the songs and drums wearing animal skins, colourful feathers and beads. As older women ululate as an accompaniment to the young people's dancing, men blow the African horn, a traditional instrument used to blow away evil spirits and invoke ancient shaman warriors.

The key message behind the celebration is the restoration of self-pride through our art forms and culture. Part of the celebration involves teaching the youth about traditional ways of living, including traditional food, and family and other values such as respect for all, young and old. The event is also marked by a display of traditional crafts and other utilities such as *thari*, the naturally treated goatskin used by mothers to carry their babies on their backs.

Specific gender roles are still called upon in preparations for ceremonies and events such as weddings and funerals. Women are often assigned the traditional role of cooking while men involve themselves with putting up the tent, collecting water and wood, as well as making the fires. Even though the roles seem separate, in reality both women and men are actively involved in ensuring the success of such festivities, and in some instances, the roles are not inflexibly divided along gender lines: men can be found participating in the cooking as well as helping to serve members of the congregation.

The church functions against a backdrop of African traditions. Mother Toloki's message is a call to appreciate the beauty of African customs. However, she actively discourages destructive practices such as *boloi* or witchcraft. According to her teachings, witchcraft has contributed to the destruction of African principles such as *letsema* and *botho/ubuntu*, which are founded on the values of mutual support, sharing, interdependence and collective as opposed to individual benefit.

The question has been rather mockingly asked why, if African people are as gifted as is claimed, they are unable to use their giftedness to help themselves? Other than being an arrogant refusal to appreciate the presence of the Supreme Being in all people of the world, a question such as this tends very conveniently to ignore the powerful role that Western countries have played in Africa's underdevelopment. According to Walter Rodney, the Guyanese scholar and activist and author of *How Europe Underdeveloped Africa*[16], the question of who is responsible for Africa's underdevelopment must be answered within the context of the role of imperialism in Africa's economic retardation. By draining Africa's wealth as well as manipulating the system, the capitalists of Europe actively extended their exploitation to all of Africa, stifling the development of Africa's

[16] Rodney, W. 1982. *How Europe Underdeveloped Africa*. Rev. ed. Washington, DC: Howard University Press.

resources. European capitalists were joined and later replaced by capitalists from the United States, which exacerbated the situation.

Walter Rodney was assassinated in the summer of 1980 amidst political turmoil in his country. His assassination was part of the global campaign against truth, justice and freedom in Africa and other developing nations. Ironically, the political and economic powerhouses behind any such campaign view their repressive acts as an expression of democracy aimed at protecting what they consider civilisation. How can we ever hope to attain freedom if we do not fight for truth? A freedom that is devoid of truth is like an unloaded AK47; it looks effective only because it carries images of power, yet it is empty. Similarly, fighting for justice without compassion is a sterile act, and the outcome will be control and domination. Without truth and compassion, the liberation that we have so bitterly fought for cannot be sustained.

Rodney was killed in an attempt to kill the truth. However, extermination of the physical channel through which truth is directed does not kill truth itself. Instead, it elevates it to the spiritual level. A bomb may have torn his body apart, but his spirit remains intact. Steve Biko and Patrice Lumumba were killed in an attempt to muzzle the truth, yet their truth lives on in the many other revolutionaries of African descent who are now working for the liberation of Africa and the Diaspora from a platform that is beyond the visible and physical.

Mother Toloki's teachings indicate that the ancestors will elevate the soul of Africans through various means, including changing *boloi* to *boloile*. The Setswana "*go loa*", like many other words within that language group, has more than one meaning. The first relates to witchcraft, while the second relates to a process of maturation that often involves fermentation. *The Oxford Modern English Dictionary*[17] defines the noun "ferment" as "agitation, excitement, tumult" while "fermentation" is explained as a chemical reaction in which an organic molecule splits into simpler substances, as in the conversion of sugar to ethyl alcohol by yeast in the making of beers, wines and spirits. This is what happens when we brew African beer. During the fermentation progresses, the beer releases unwanted elements in the form of gases until it is ultimately declared "ripe" and ready for consumption.

In the same way, *boloi* will undergo fermentation, releasing negative energies in the process, and ultimately being transformed into *boloile* and serving as a powerfully positive, spiritually uplifting and human-enhancing African medicine for the soul. *Polao e fetoga kalafi*, darkness gives way to light. Just as the destructive powers of African witchcraft will not be allowed to flourish, the oppressive powers of white witchcraft on the black psyche will be rooted out. Africa will be given new eyes; Africa's vision will be restored. Africa will think, look and act differently because of having undergone fermentation.

South Africa is asked to lead the way, to embrace Mother Toloki's teachings. This call is made very clear in the following passage from a spiritual message entitled *"Kgolagano ya Basweu le bantsho*, "Reconciliation between whites and blacks", written at half past five on the morning of 26 August 1989:

Ahee, Batho Ma-Afrika, batho mokgethiwa o ka re ke ditoro. Nako ya goroswa, basweu ba tlhakatlhakana,

[17] *The Oxford Modern English Dictionary.* 1992. Oxford: Clarendon Press: p.386.

baetapele ba naga ba latlhegelwa ke tsela, ba garumana, ba betsana ka noga e tshela. Lefatshe lotlhe la duma, matlho otlhe a leba lefatsheng South Africa.

From all corners of the world, spiritual leaders are calling for a return to the Source. Many indigenous theologians are searching for a religion that integrates the ancient teachings of their communities. Women theologians pray for a matriarchal interpretation of the Bible. All these paths are interconnected; they are all part of a whole.

Following a period of incubation mistaken for darkness, Africa is called to give light. Because of having experienced war and genocide, we will teach peace and respect for human life. Because we know what poverty and disease look like, we will not wish them on anyone. Because of knowing first-hand the suffering that comes with colonisation and repression, we will fight for a government ruled not by fear but by truth, love and compassion.

May we be led as we lead.

New beginnings

Journal entry: 01.01.01.

It's a brand new day, a new month, a new year and a new century. A new life too. I am in Venda, a place where African legends reside. Magnificent mountains and valleys surround me. Everywhere I look, I see life. My ears are tuned to sounds; harmonious and chaotic sounds that signify life. Each bird sings its own distinctive melody. Crickets chirp, unwilling to be outdone by the birdsong. To the human ear, the sounds seem unco-ordinated. To the spiritual ear, however, they are the song of balance and harmony. The sights, sounds, and scents are one in this exquisite part of Africa nestled in the Soutpansberg Mountains.

Looking out at the mountains, I wonder what stories they would tell. Which African healers and prophets lived in them? Who were the warriors who once used this mountain range as a fortress in times of war? Isn't it amazing that more often than not, stories of Africa are stories of war? As a people, we have experienced such brutality. Our spirits are broken as a result. Yet, it is in the broken spirit that we witness the tenacity and resilience of the human condition. We have conquered. We have also been conquered. Yet, we can recover from our past. We are a spiritual people, an interconnected, beautiful and intelligent people.

This century is called the African century. This century is a time to weep, a time to confront our broken spirit and heal. It has taken us time to complete the cycle by returning political power to indigenous African leaders. It has taken us 37 years from the era of Kwame Nkrumah to Rolihlahla Mandela. Over time, we have realised that the mere transfer of political power away from colonial empires does not necessarily translate into liberation. It is instead the beginning of a painful process of healing; a process of reclaiming who we were prior to being bewitched into believing that our worth was determined by the colour of our skin, and into not seeing that our colour is the colour of the earth. For a very long time, we believed that our intelligence was as long as a strand of our hair without realising that like our hair, an African way of life is convoluted in its simplicity.

It is a time to recover our wisdom, a time to reclaim our ability to love and be loved. A time to return, *Maropeng go a boelwa*. Only if we can do that can we unlock the wisdom embodied in Africa, in the prophets, storytellers, poets, writers, astronomers, scientists and economists of Africa, in the architects who created the pyramids. Then we will be able to reclaim the intelligence of our unlettered philosophers who continue to hold their earth summits in a circle under a baobab or *morula* tree. Then we will be able to plant our minds with their wisdom and teachings. We will live our truth, reminded by Ngugi wa Thiongo that we are not a wasteland of non-achievement but victims of cultural imperialism. Yet you are a victim only for as long as you hold on to that status. We have gone full circle; this is the time to reconnect and recover.

Talking about victims brings me back to my life. There have been times in the past when I have held others responsible for my life. I have blamed others and external forces for the way my life turned out. Yet I have the power to shape my life, to make it what I want it to be. From this beautiful setting on this amazing morning, I welcome yet another reminder that I am fully responsible for my own happiness. I have evolved with time. Like a sculpture, I am a magnificent work of art in the making.

I commit to a way of life that is gentle and loving. Thank you, Lord, for having assigned a star to watch over me when my way was dark. Glory be to my ancestors for their constant and consistent love. A new life beckons and I will embrace it. Where the spirits of the mighty continent of Africa lead, I shall follow.

I am emerging.

Emerging from a war
a warrior can be choked
by peace.
Emerging from the dark
A pilgrim can be blinded
By light
Emerging from repression
A slave can be paralysed
By hate and revenge.
As we emerge
from a turbulent past
Let there be light
And love.

MORENA LE BADIMO, BOLOKA SETSHABA SA ETSHO
AMEN.

The time is ripe

It is Thursday, 15 November 2001 and as usual I am in Acornhoek, teaching and learning from rural women. This gathering is different, though, because almost all of the women in the room are knowingly living positively with the HI virus. They are full of life. They are determined to live their lives well in spite of their daily dose of discrimination, physical discomfort and poverty. The way they live their lives makes so many of the problems that many of us regard as challenging or life threatening seem trivial

I notice with the deepest humility that what these women have to deal with almost defies description. I listen and watch quietly as they talk of poverty and violence. With a lump in my throat, I hear how some of them are forced to breast-feed their babies because they have no money to buy formula. I watch with deep sorrow as one of the babies sucks her mother's infected milk. I listen as they describe how some are forced to insert chemicals in their vaginas to avoid being assaulted by their partners for being "wet" and therefore for "sleeping around".

As human beings, how and why did we choose to go against nature in this way? Was it through ignorance, or the desire to assert power as a way of demeaning another? Vaginal and penile secretions are natural, designed to make the sex act pleasurable. I shudder to think of the implications of this situation for the spread of HIV. A brutalised vagina is not just a prescription for painful sex, but also increases the likelihood of minor lacerations which will provide easy access for the virus, particularly when so many men refuse to use a condom.

There are no words to describe the intensity of the pain in that room. It was acute enough to cut a human heart wide open. I listened and watched them tell their stories without a hint of self-pity or the intention of giving up on themselves. Despite the pain and the suffering, I sensed their determination to live life in the best way they can. At that moment I heard a voice in my heart saying: "You belong here. This is where you need to be". I looked up through the prism of my tears and saw blurred visions of new beginnings. I knew at that moment that it was time for me to move from Johannesburg to seek a meaningful life with these women as my teachers and role models. My decision was not just motivated by the fact that I wanted to help, but also inspired by a yearning to receive an education about African life, its culture and philosophies, from ordinary but wise women and men in my land. My move was not just driven by the fact that I have a lot to teach. I wanted to learn how to live a life, to search for who I really am, led by these unlettered and uncertificated Africans whose stories do not appear on the pages of the textbooks used by their children in institutions of learning. There is so much to learn from our own people, yet we remain content to internalise the words and emulate the actions of strangers in distant and foreign lands. I had dreamt before about facilitating workshops and disseminating wisdom gathered from our elders in our languages. And now the time was ripe.

The next day, Friday, 16 November, I drove back to Johannesburg, having found a school for my children and having had a brief meeting with Rina Venter, an estate agent, about finding a place to stay in White River. I told the teachers at the school that I had decided on the move the previous day and that my children did not know anything about it. They all thought I was brave, if a little crazy, and they gave me caps, bumper stickers and other material about the school for the children. I arrived at home late that night, and found them waiting for me, as though they knew that something was about to turn their lives around. I told them about the workshop and my deep longing to work with rural women, and asked them to think my proposed plans over and tell me honestly how they felt the next day.

In a way, the timing was perfect. It was the end of the year and they would start at a new school in the new year. I had sold my house the previous month and was intending to move anyway. I had known I wanted out, but didn't know where I would go. I had had enough of a soulless life in a big city. I had wanted to move closer to the earth, and the mountains of Mpumalanga were reaching out to me. Everything seemed to be falling in place.

The next morning, Saturday, I got up early and drove to Kgomo Kgomo to share my plan with my parents. I expected resistance, yet to my surprise both my mother and father were thrilled. They had watched me struggle to find my essence for many years, and over the past year in particular, and they so much wanted me to sign off and rejuvenate. Without any reservations, they blessed my plans.

As a sign of respect for custom, my mother accompanied me to my aunt, *Mme* Morongwa, to ask the ancestors to bless the move. We were not sure whether this request was going to be granted, and so I was overjoyed when my aunt kissed me on the cheek and happily announced that my life's tribulations were about to end. Further confirmation that the time was ripe! I had tried moving before, but on those occasions my path was not blessed. My earlier reasons for moving had been different, though: I had been running away from the gift. There had been teaching jobs in Cape Town and Durban, a scholarship to study development studies at Sussex University, and a research fellowship at Rutgers University in the USA. On each of these occasions something had happened close to my departure and thwarted my plans. I had wanted to run, but could not. In hindsight, it was because I needed to learn the necessary lessons first. I needed clarity as to who is in me, before me, behind me and around me before I could be allowed to move away from the Source. I had to understand that the gift is a part of who I am and that it will therefore follow me wherever I go.

I drove back home exhilarated. I had two weeks to find a new home, pack up my belongings and my children, and head off to a new life. The following Friday, 23 November, I was back in Mpumalanga, taking the children for their school admission interviews and looking for a home. The move was scheduled for 30 November, the Friday after that.

I spent my birthday, 29 November, packing boxes. Early on the Friday morning, Katlego and I loaded our van with paper and cans to deliver to a school recycling project and a few other smaller household goods to deliver in Soweto. We then headed south on the highway, intending to beat the morning traffic and be back home in time for the removal truck.

On the way, Katlego and I had the time to share some thoughts. He confessed that he had not been himself over the past year and had found himself easily influenced by his peers. He said that he lacked focus at school and sometimes felt empty and unloved. I, in turn, acknowledged my failures and limitations as a single mother and apologised for the times I had let him down. I realised that my spiritual and emotional turbulence and lack of inner peace had affected him, and I thanked him for being a part of my life, for being there for me during my trials and tribulations, without asking for much in return. I promised to love him, always. He thanked me for my love even when he felt unworthy of it. With tears in our eyes, we declared our commitment to each other. We both felt ready for a new life.

At that moment Katlego looked back, and saw that the bookcase that we were transporting was sliding around on the back of the van. I slowed down and stopped on the grass verge a safe distance beyond the emergency lane and he got out to tie the bookcase down securely. In the driver's seat I smiled for a moment, grateful for a child like him and full of hope. And then the unthinkable happened. A car travelling on the highway lost control and ploughed into us. Katlego was flung several metres, and the van rolled, narrowly avoiding plummeting down an embankment. As I was flung from side to side I was conscious, yet helpless to control my fate. I remember praying aloud.

When the van came to a standstill, I sat, dazed and silent, trying to work out what had happened, with blood pouring from my scalp and nose. I tried to open the door, but could not. Fortunately, some other motorists had stopped and they helped me out of the car. Wincing in pain from an injured leg, I went in search of my son. I found him lying motionless in the grass. Despite my past nursing training, I didn't even have the presence of mind to feel his pulse or check his breathing. He lay soaked in a pool of blood, and I feared the worst.

I found my cell phone and called my family. Someone called an ambulance. The police arrived, tow trucks pulled up, more people came across, cars slowed down to look. I couldn't believe what was happening, I could not understand. Why? Why now? Why me?

Less than 30 minutes after the accident, as I knelt beside my son, I looked up to see my brother Jimmy running towards us, having abandoned his car on the side of the road because of the traffic. My vision blurred by the tears in my eyes, I watched my brother fly towards me, the embodiment of love in a suit and a colourful tie. I saw love running towards me. I saw love with my very own eyes.

Once he reached us, he hugged me and assured me that everything would be alright. I believed him. But then I had to deal with two tow truck drivers hell bent on making me sign a document whose contents I had neither the time nor the inclination to read. From the moment I managed to get out of my car, they had been following me around asking me for a signature. I asked them what it was for and they said something like third party insurance. How heartless and unscrupulous could these people be? My son had suffered who knows what injuries, I was anxiously waiting for an ambulance, and all they were concerned about was preying on my vulnerability and making sure that I signed on the dotted line. Couldn't this have waited until my son had been attended to? I was confused, certainly, but not confused enough to be fooled by two white tow truck drivers. There was no way that I was going to sign any document at that moment. I experienced a rush of mistrust, and in that moment their whiteness was all that I saw. Yes, indeed, it is in moments of deep crisis that latent perceptions resurface. The ambulance arrived and I was very happy to leave my brother to deal with these two *okes*. Good Lord, we have been afraid of the white man for far too long.

After being stabilised, my son was put in the back of the ambulance while I sat in the front. Because of his head injuries, he was in extreme pain and less than co-operative with the ambulance personnel as they attempted to put up a drip. I saw frustration in their eyes and I heard them swear. I was asked whether I had medical aid, and if so, which one? I did not have any health insurance myself, but Katlego was covered by my ex-husband's medical aid, which meant he would have access to quality care. In the same ambulance lay an injured man who had no medical aid. He had been picked up from where he had been injured and driven all the way to our accident scene, where we were attended to first and driven to a private hospital; only then was he taken to a public health facility, where he in all likelihood spent hours waiting to be seen. All that time, he lay quietly in pain, not even looking in our direction.

When we arrived at the hospital, I got out to follow my son. My face swollen, my clothes soaked in blood and unable to walk, I was asked at the entrance whether I was one of that hospital's patients, meaning could I afford to pay? I tried to explain that my son was injured and that I needed to be with him, but the emergency room nurse was not interested. "Are you," she asked again, "also *our* patient?" I said no, wondering whether she was going to turn me away and send me off with the ambulance while they attended to my son. Luckily, one of the Nightingales who was listening nearby brought a wheelchair and insisted that I be wheeled to the waiting room until my family arrived.

Less than two hours after the accident, I had my family around me. So much care, so much love. After my family assured the hospital staff that they would pay for my treatment, I was attended to by a doctor and sent for X-rays. I had sustained soft tissue injuries to my chest and knee and a fractured nasal bone. My scalp lacerations were sutured and I was given a prescription for pain tablets and a set of crutches.

We were told that Katlego was unconscious in intensive care and that he would have to have surgery in the afternoon. We were kept waiting until the last moment for a neurologist and an orthopaedic surgeon to explain to us what was wrong. The nurses had been instructed to ask me to sign a consent form, but they were reluctant to have me sign it before meeting with and hearing from the doctors. At last, the doctors spared me a few moments and hurriedly explained the extent of my son's injuries and why he needed surgery. I was struck by how little time they were prepared to spend with me, how rushed the communication at a time when they should have acknowledged me as a mother and a human being.

That first day at the hospital was a complete nightmare. We stayed on in the waiting room even after Katlego went to surgery. We did not know how long it was going to take, and we could not go home. One of the nurses in the intensive care unit was extremely kind and concerned. She urged us to go home and promised to call as soon as my son came back from surgery. She was also adamant that I should rest, yet I found rest impossible.

When I agreed to a new life, I did not mean it to include having my son lying unconscious on a respirator for days with a fractured skull and bleeding on the brain. My vision did not include my son suffering a collapsed lung, swelling of the heart, a broken femur and amputated toes. When I said I was ready to move, I did not intend my household goods to be stored in a warehouse somewhere in Johannesburg while I watched over my child in hospital.

I had put the move out of my mind completely, but then I got a call from the removal company to say that the new owners of my house were impatient and that they were tossing my belongings out into the garden. Earlier in the day, I had phoned the estate agent to tell him about the accident and to ask if we could delay the move until the next day. He and the new occupants said they were sorry about the accident, but insisted that business was business. According to the contract, we had agreed to move out that day, and that day it was going to be. The new owners' mother, they said, was arriving from Europe the next evening and they had already planned a housewarming party for her. My son was fighting for his life in hospital and the new occupants couldn't wait a mere 24 hours because they had already planned a party!

I later phoned Rina Venter, the estate agent in White River, and explained that I would not be coming, and that I was not even sure whether I would still be moving to the Lowveld. She offered me words of comfort, and encouraged me to stay strong and keep the faith, and not to worry about the house for the moment. She promised to pray for me. She and I have been close ever since. My close association with this older Afrikaans woman has made me review the African principle of *botho*, and I have since concluded that it is not necessarily an exclusively African, but a universal human phenomenon. I know of Africans who publicly preach the African Renaissance and *ubuntu*, but are incapable of honouring their fellow human beings. I know of leaders who preach and know all the African teachings by heart, yet walk parallel to the truth. I have had encounters with well-known proponents of Africa's rebirth who will barely greet you, even though greetings are so central to being African. I have learnt that the one thing that I have to do to change the world is to change myself. Iyanla Vanzant believes that if you want something, give it. If you want something, give it. Such a simple principle, yet I so wish that someone would whisper it in the ear of some of our national and global leaders.

Katlego's hospitalisation was a time of great challenge and immense growth for me.

Every single day, my mother, my siblings and I visited the hospital, hoping to find him awake. My ex-husband, Moloele, who is a medical doctor, worked day and night monitoring Katlego's situation. He could easily have chosen not to be there, but he was. He worked tirelessly and gave his compassion abundantly. My family and I have not words enough to thank him and his wife for the gift of love they gave to Katlego in hospital.

As the minutes, the hours and days slipped by, I felt my faith and hope slowly slipping away from me. One morning, while my mother and I were at Katlego's bedside, watching his ashen face as the respirator breathed for him, my mother spoke to him as she always did, and at the same time called on the ancestors to return him to us. Despite this, I felt myself accepting my son's imminent death. I was in a sacred and private conversation with my spirits when my mother sharply reprimanded me for letting him go. Had she been reading my mind? How else would she have known what I was thinking?

A moment later, I felt my strength return. My sacred vessels were refilled with immense faith and my spiritual muscles pumped with incredible power. I felt strong again. Deep down, though, I knew that what I had just experienced was incredible. I had felt what it is like to let go of someone whom you truly love, someone who is an irreplaceable part of who you are. I had learnt the lesson of detachment. The feeling was momentary, but deeply profound.

On leaving the hospital we phoned my father to tell him that we were on our way home to find strength and solace from the Source. We found him and *Mme* Morongwa at Bollantlokwe. We were blessed on that day with a prayer and a ritual that we had never witnessed or experienced before. My father was awfully quiet and his eyes were puffy and red. I knew that he too was afraid that Katlego might die. In fact, he confessed later that when we had called to say we were coming, he had thought to himself *"Ngwana ngwanaka o ile"* and begun planning a funeral in his head.

The next day *Mme* Morongwa came with us to the hospital. She and my mother surrounded my son with love and filled his soul with prayer. They called on the ancestors to give him back to us. During this time, I waited outside. When the elders engage in a spiritual pilgrimage, the younger ones like me wait and pray in anticipation of an unknown outcome. *Ke tiro e e masisi, e batla bagolo*. Even though I was Katlego's mother and had carried him in my womb, the plea for his life to be returned had to be uttered by those who had carried me in their womb. We left the hospital quietly, calmly and full of hope. And we found him awake the next day. He was confused and disoriented, but conscious. You have to believe in miracles to experience them. Believe in them to experience them rather than experiencing them first and only then believing.

Throughout my son's hospitalisation and my recuperation, my mother was with me, helping me to bath, making sure that I ate, slept and prayed. She was the one who helped me to get up in the morning, always in anticipation of a miracle. She gave me refresher courses in mothering in preparation for what I would have to do once my son was discharged. I remember feeling afraid of letting my son down, wondering whether I would be able to take care of him as well as my mother had taken care of me. I also had to recognise and own a latent fear of accessing and caring for the masculine. But once he was discharged, I was ready. He was physically emaciated and spiritually drained, and I was determined to cook for him and to love him back to health. I was ready to be a full-time mother again.

With Katlego discharged, I had to review my earlier decisions. I had no home, and I had no idea whether my furniture was safe. I had left my previous home on the morning of the accident, and I wondered whether I still had a place to stay in White River. I was not even sure whether I still wanted to move, particularly once I learnt how much it had cost to store my things. I decided not to go ahead with the move to the Lowveld, and informed my parents. My father disagreed, saying that when the ancestors had blessed the move, they had also known about the accident. When they agreed that I should go, they also knew that I was going to be tested – again. In looking back at this moment of my life, I am reminded of these beautiful words from Paulo Coelho's *The Alchemist*: "before a dream is realized, the Soul of the World tests everything that was learned along the way. It does this not because it is evil, but so that we can, in addition to realizing our dreams, master the lessons we've learned as we've moved toward that dream. That's the point at which most people give up. It's the point at which, as we say in the language of the desert, one 'dies of thirst just when the palm trees have appeared on the horizon'".[18]

To this day, there are times when I look at my son and I am choked with emotion and disbelief. I received an e-mail from Julie Oyegun, a friend in Washington DC, saying that it is not often that our children are given back to us. I couldn't agree more. My life will never be the same again. Katlego says his life has changed too. We are a team, and we are alive.

I am back in rural South Africa, pursuing my education and my dream of learning the teachings of my people. It is in my yesterday that I will make sense of my today in preparation for tomorrow.

like the magnificent carvings of Kilimanjaro
the teachings of my people
are solid and permanent
if etched in my soul

like power of the water at Mosi oa Thunya
the teachings of my people

[18] Coelho, P. 1999. *The Alchemist*. London: HarperCollins: p.139.

are complex yet simple
if highlighted in my vision

like footprints on the dunes of Kgalagadi
the teachings of my people
can be lost to the wind
if not held in my breath

my people's footprints
if not made solid and permanent
once blown by the wind
can never be recovered.

Where are we heading? There is a saying in Setswana: *"Mo tlhako ya pele e gatileng, ya morago le yona e tla gata"*. The ancient Chinese also tell us that a journey of a thousand miles begins with one step. If we are ever going to master the art of tracking our ancestors' thousand footprints, we need to stop running and pay attention. Without one mindful step at a time, we may not make it. Mindfulness involves a willingness to accept the humble position of being used as a spiritual channel. I have finally had to accept that I myself am nothing, I know nothing, I own nothing and no one (not even my children), and that the Holy Spirit will work through me with or without my permission.